The
Compleat
Therapist

The
Compleat
Therapist

JEFFREY A. KOTTLER

Jossey-Bass Publishers

San Francisco   •   Oxford   •   1991

THE COMPLEAT THERAPIST
by Jeffrey A. Kottler

Copyright © 1991 by: Jossey-Bass Inc., Publishers
350 Sansome Street
San Francisco, California 94104
&
Jossey-Bass Limited
Headington Hill Hall
Oxford OX3 0BW

Library of Congress Cataloging-in-Publication Data

Kottler, Jeffrey A.
   The compleat therapist / Jeffrey A. Kottler.
     p.   cm. — (The Jossey-Bass social and behavioral science
series)
   Includes bibliographical references.
   Includes index.
   ISBN 1-55542-302-7 (alk. paper)
   1. Psychotherapy.   I. Title.   II. Series.
   [DNLM: 1. Psychotherapy — methods.   WM 420 K865c]
   RC480.K667   1991
   616.89'14 — dc20
   DNLM/DLC   90-5197
   for Library of Congress   CIP

Manufactured in the United States of America

The paper in this book meets the guidelines for
permanence and durability of the Committee on
Production Guidelines for Book Longevity of the
Council on Library Resources.

JACKET DESIGN BY WILLI BAUM

FIRST EDITION

Code 9103

THE JOSSEY-BASS
SOCIAL AND BEHAVIORAL SCIENCE SERIES

Contents

Preface

I have a confession. I have been practicing, teaching, and writing about psychotherapy for over fifteen years and I still do not know how and why it really works. Do not misunderstand me: I know what to *say* about therapy to clients and students, who would be very upset if they thought I could not explain what I was doing. I say therapy is a mysterious process. I tell them it works differently for each person. I explain that it is based on a trusting relationship in which we explore your life in depth and help you to come to terms with unresolved issues and make some decisions regarding where you are headed. We create a plan to get you what you want.

Most people seem to accept that explanation. And I breathe a sigh of relief. It took one belligerent client to force this confession out of me.

"Sir, with all due respect, if *that* is why therapy works, how come the previous therapist I saw told me it was because my family structure needed to be realigned, another I consulted said it empowers me — whatever *that* means — and still another mentioned something about retraining my cognitive patterns?"

Good question, huh? It so happens that I have been asking myself that very question all these years. I started out in my professional life as an avid Freudian. I loved the complexity of psychoanalysis, its poetry, and its regimented system. I felt safe in the company of peers who all spoke the same language and helped one another stay on track. I felt it worked well, too; it seemed to help people gain a clearer perspective on their lives.

One influential supervisor urged me to explore more fully the simplicity of client-centered counseling when Carl Rogers was the rage. To my utter amazement, I found that dealing with client feelings was indeed a powerful way to work! I abandoned Freud (or at least swore off theoretical monogamy) during the "touchie-feelie" days of encounter groups.

Another mentor introduced me to behavior therapy and the value of helping clients set realistic goals. If I had reduced attention to the unconscious, defenses, transference, repressed feelings, I could be forgiven — my clients made definable progress in leaps and bounds! Although I no longer dealt very much with past conflicts, or even present feelings, my clients improved by focusing on specific behaviors they wished to change.

In my doctoral program, I took an advanced practicum in rational-emotive therapy. This was a time when Albert Ellis, Aaron Beck, and other cognitive-based theorists were making their mark. I eventually became a full-fledged disciple. I read all the books, went to workshops religiously, and practiced RET exclusively for over a year. I seemed to thrive on the provocative confrontational style of countering irrational beliefs — and so did my clients. I eventually let go of rational-emotive therapy. Although it worked with my clients, I felt so constricted repeating the same injunctions and interventions over and over.

When Ericksonian hypnosis, strategic therapy, and neurolinguistic programming hit the professional scene, they were a breath of fresh air. How could I have been so negligent all these years in dealing only with individual issues and ignoring family dynamics and linguistic structures? I attempted to rectify my lapses by mastering these new helping strategies and, again to my delight, discovered they worked like magic.

Was it because I longed for more intimacy in my work, more depth to my sessions, that I came full circle back to an insight-oriented, existential style? Or was it because once I entered private practice, I needed the security of long-term clients? In either case, I had retained a bit of each of the approaches I had, at one time, practiced. I was now more flexible and had more options. My clients seemed to improve, maybe even more than before, but I believe that was more a function of my experience than of which theory I was practicing.

I do not wish to sound cavalier or flippant in my everchanging search for the optimal therapeutic approach. Because I have intensively studied and enthusiastically practiced a number of different therapies, I feel motivated to take a step back from parochial ideology to find the inlaid patterns hidden from view. For I am still perplexed by how it is possible that these theories (and a dozen others), which advocate doing such dramatically different things, could all be helpful. How does therapy work if it can be practiced by competent professionals in such diverse ways?

Contents of the Book

This is a book about what works in psychotherapy. I present a synthesis of the best features in most systems of practice and a unified portrait of the consummate practitioner that transcends theoretical allegiances. It is an attempt to find the essence of what makes a therapist, *any* therapist, most effective.

This book is the third installment of a trilogy that began with *On Being a Therapist,* an exploration of how clinicians are affected by their work with clients; continues with *The Imperfect Therapist,* a study of how clinicians handle feelings of failure; and ends with the present publication, which examines what consistently works for successful practitioners.

Whereas the previous two books in this series have dealt with many of the stresses and challenges that are so much a part of therapeutic work, *The Compleat Therapist* carries a more inspirational message: that it is possible to synthesize what constitutes "good" therapy and identify the characteristics, qualities, and skills that are most likely to lead to positive outcomes.

From questionnaires, in-depth interviews with practitioners, a comprehensive review of the literature, as well as my own personal experience, I have attempted to answer several important questions. What makes a therapist most effective? How can it be possible that practitioners who seem to be doing such different things are all helpful? What do most successful clinicians have in common in terms of their thinking processes, personal qualities, and skills? What more can we do to pool our knowledge and experience to create a new age of cooperation and synthesis in the practice of psychotherapy?

The first section of *The Compleat Therapist* contains three chapters that explore in depth the commonalities of most therapeutic approaches. Chapter One describes one of the most perplexing paradoxes of our profession: how therapists can do distinctly different things in their work and yet still produce similar results. The first chapter introduces the major topics of the book, including the shared themes that are part of any therapeutic encounter.

Chapter Two reviews the historical as well as current efforts in the field to integrate diverse therapeutic approaches into a unified model. This perspective helps us to appreciate just how daunting is the task of trying to reconcile discrepant and contradictory variables with a synthesis of what we know and understand, especially when we cannot even reach a consensus on language and concepts. Chapter Three operationalizes the work of eclectic/pragmatic/integrative theorists and practitioners by reviewing the variables that are common to all effective psychotherapies.

The second section of the book examines more specifically the attributes that are part of a therapist's optimal functioning. Regardless of espoused theoretical allegiances, professional disciplines, or style of operation, effective therapists share certain qualities (Chapter Four), thinking processes (Chapter Five), and skills (Chapter Six). These identifiable behaviors and processes that are part of any effective therapist's repertoire, regardless of how they are labeled by various schools, help explain why so many fine clinicians can appear to be doing such different things and yet still help clients to change and grow.

The concluding chapter develops the reader's ability to personalize the many ideas contained in this book so that he or she can maintain the challenges and joys of effective practice. The *compleat* therapist, from the archaic version of *complete,* connoting the highest level of attainment in any field, is the ultimate goal to which we all aspire.

Acknowledgments

My thanks to the following therapists who consented to be interviewed, or who shared their views on what being effective means to them: Norbert Birnbaum, Diane Blau, Robert Brown, Brian Connolley, Gerald Corey, Karen Eversole, Maryann Greenstone, Maryalice Marshall, Peter Martin, Clark Moustakas, Edward Nol, Heather Pietryka, Natalie Rice, Kathleen Ritter, Deborah Snyder, Lora Valataro, William Van Hoose, Orlando Villegas, John Vriend, Diane Webb, and Gail Williams.

I also wish to express my gratitude to the following individuals who reviewed the manuscript and provided many helpful suggestions regarding its structure and content: Barry Farber, William Henry, John Norcross, and Constance Shapiro.

I dedicate this book to the two most supportive people I know: my wife, Ellen Kottler, and my editor, Gracia A. Alkema, who embody the qualities I most admire in any compleat therapist or human being.

Charleston, South Carolina   Jeffrey A. Kottler
December 1990

The Author

JEFFREY A. KOTTLER has studied at Oakland University, Harvard University, Wayne State University, and the University of Stockholm, and received his Ph.D. degree from the University of Virginia. He has worked as a therapist in a variety of settings including hospitals, mental health centers, schools, clinics, universities, corporations, and private practice. He has lectured extensively throughout North and South America and served as a Fulbright Scholar in Peru establishing counseling programs in underdeveloped regions.

Kottler is the author or coauthor of *Ethical and Legal Issues in Counseling and Psychotherapy* (1977), *Pragmatic Group Leadership* (1983), *Introduction to Therapeutic Counseling* (1985), *On Being a Therapist* (1986), *The Imperfect Therapist: Learning from Failure in Therapeutic Practice* (1989), and *Private Moments, Secret Selves: Enriching Our Time Alone* (1990). He is currently an associate professor of counseling at The Citadel in Charleston, South Carolina.

The
Compleat
Therapist

CHAPTER ONE

How Therapists Can Do
Such Different Things
and Still Get Similar Results

Why are some therapists generally helpful and some are not? Journals and books are full of plausible explanations, ranging from the frequency of using certain interventions to the presence of particular interpersonal factors. And yet, while theoreticians, researchers, and practitioners argue among themselves about what exactly makes a difference — which elements, variables, qualities, processes, concepts, behaviors, and attitudes — clients are remarkably clear about what they want and need in their helpers. Generally, they prefer someone who is warm and approachable, someone who listens to and understands them. They want a professional who is competent and confident, who gives them a sense of hope. They want an active collaborator in the process. They want someone who they perceive to be like themselves, but not too similar. They favor a helper who is also emotionally healthy. And they prefer an expert who is perceived as having power, status, and prestige. In short, clients have definite ideas about what they want in their helpers, even if they do not know what they want in their lives.

A Client Looks at Three Therapists

During the writing of this book I experienced what I believe was a mid-life transition. I began to feel restless with my life,

1

confused as to what I wanted to do next, and somewhat unhappy with the progress I was making on my own. I was feeling anxious, and then once I began exploring options, I started
feeling depressed by what I perceived were limited possibilities.
What I was living through had all the hallmarks of what I recognized as a developmental crisis.

I became indecisive. I found it difficult to concentrate. And
yet, I suppose like most prospective consumers of therapy, I
made up a bunch of excuses for why I could handle this on my
own. I am a therapist, after all . . . and a pretty good one. I
should be able to help myself through this, just as I have lived
through it with so many clients. Finally, I rationalized to myself that this would make good research for the book I was writing. (What is the use of being a therapist if it does not help us
to invent good rationalizations?) All in the interest of science,
I could visit several different therapists and see what makes them
effective, actually *experience* the effects of what they do. Hey,
maybe I would even find it personally helpful.

I scheduled appointments with three different therapists in
the same week, unwilling to trust just one. I figured I could see
what each of them was like and decide who was the best for me.
My first awareness after taking this initial step was already how
much better I felt. Clients, of course, have said this to me all
the time, but I had not realized just what they meant. (It has
been many years since my last therapy experience as a client.)
I noticed myself doing a lot of rehearsing of how I would present
myself and what I would say. It was hard to sit back, relax,
wait, and trust the process I purport to believe in and teach to
others. It was a test of faith.

Dr. Genghis. The first therapist was a small man in a cavern-
ous office. Trained originally as a psychiatrist and analyst, Dr.
Genghis's office had many of the trappings I would expect in
such a setting—big desk, swoon couch, separate entrances. Very
formal. Yet I did not for a moment expect I would be seeing
a conventional analyst . . . and I was not disappointed.

Before I even got my bearings and settled in my chair, he
was on me like a predator. He asked me some questions but

did not like my answers. It took him about five minutes to size me up and give me his assessment. And it was brutal. I reeled from the accusation that I was essentially irresponsible. I tried to process what he was saying, but by then he had leveled several more rounds. My back was drenched with sweat. I was smiling like an idiot, stammering out my protests of disagreement.

"It's simple," he says. "You don't want to grow up."

"Well, that *could* be true, but . . . ."

"See, even now you intellectualize. You talk around things. You don't say what you mean."

Gosh, he *was* right about that. Maybe the other stuff is true, too. And if so, then everything I thought about myself is false. I am not who I am, but someone else I do not know.

I could see where he was taking me and I did not like it one bit. If I stayed in treatment with him I would become more responsible, more like him, and what *he* views is appropriate conduct for a man my age. Shame on me for wanting to change aspects of my life that were not broken — all to placate some silly dream I will never reach.

"Kottler, when are you going to stop this nonsense, stop running away, and start facing yourself?"

I was devastated. My knees felt like rubber; I could barely walk. I sat in my car for an hour trying to recover from the onslaught. In some ways he really had me pegged. But could it *all* be true?

Clearly, I was genuinely moved by this experience. I cannot recall, ever, spending a more frightening hour in my life. I felt beat up, bruised, and yet it was a "good" ache. I was even telling myself: "Boy, that was fun!" like a kid who screamed in terror all the way through a roller coaster ride, stumbles off in tears, and then says, "Let's do that again!"

The question was, should I go back? A part of me was so intrigued by his bluntness and assaults on what I thought was my reality. And another part of me thought he was a lunatic. He was everything I have always wanted *not* to be as a therapist. He was neither warm nor accepting; in fact he was extremely critical and judgmental. He did not deal with my feelings nor did he work with me in areas that I preferred. He ignored my desires. He ridiculed my defenses. He called me names. He was quite simply the meanest bastard I had ever met. So, how could I even dream of going back for more? What did he do that was so effective?

It certainly was not his sweet disposition and kindness. He did not exactly inspire me to trust him. Everything I confided in him he turned against me. He was, at times, cruel and impatient, going for the jugular when I was already disoriented and vulnerable. I did not feel heard or understood.

So what *did* he do that helped me? And I truly felt helped, although at the time I could not exactly say how. Obviously, he was a master at shaking me up, helping me to feel uncomfortable with myself and thereby prodding me. I absolutely loved his stunning honesty and I appreciated his directness. I also got a kick out of his eccentric style — he had me enthralled by the force and power of his personality. Heck, I did not agree with much of what he had to say, but I liked the show he put on.

I just knew I would get my money's worth with Dr. Genghis. I liked the way he knew how to get to me so quickly. His intuition about some things was remarkable. At one point he asked me what my earliest memory was. I described, at age three, carrying my brother home from the hospital after he was born. He asked me how I *felt* in the memory, and I replied: terrified. He asked me what I was so afraid of. "Why, of the responsibility. What if I dropped him?"

Dr. Genghis looked at me with those vulturous, beady eyes and said, "Of course! Can't you hear yourself? Since age three you have been terrified of responsibility."

Well, whether this interpretation was accurate or not, it sure got my attention. It got me thinking in new ways. He touched me in a way that I still cannot forget.

Dr. Glinda. I must say that I was feeling somewhat leery about showing up for my scheduled appointment with the next therapist the following day. As so many clients say to themselves: maybe I do not need therapy after all. I found myself making up the same feeble excuses I hear every day — that it is too costly, too time consuming, that I am too old to change my ways or too seasoned to fall for the tricks of the trade. This last remark was especially revealing of my underlying skepticism and mistrust of the process that I have devoted my life to believing in . . . for others.

In spite of my apprehensions, by this time I *really* needed professional help just to recover from the first experience. Dr. Glinda was as different from Dr. Genghis as two therapists could be. Everything he was not, she was. And vice versa. She was warm, approachable, quite loving and caring. I felt unnerved by her look. It was as if she knew some deep, dark secrets about me too, but unlike Dr. Genghis, she was not going to share them yet.

We spent most of the session talking about the meaning of the previous session with Genghis. She asked me how I felt about changing my basic nature: "How does it feel to have an expert tell you that you don't know what's good for yourself?"

Dr. Glinda did everything I would have done for myself if I had walked into my office as a client. She listened closely. She supported me. She reinforced the idea that I *did* know what was best. Well, this was just what I wanted to hear. Maybe I would not have to grow up after all!

I found Dr. Glinda to be effective in most senses of what I would expect from a therapist. She heard me and understood what I wanted from her at that moment (although she may have been colluding with my resistance). It certainly was not nearly as frightening to work with her. I felt safe in her presence. She seemed to genuinely care about me. She would go at *my* pace rather than hers. I decided this was also someone who could help me, but in a way profoundly different from Dr. Genghis.

Dr. Wright. The first thing that struck me about the third therapist I consulted was his smile—he seemed so natural and inviting. Dr. Wright appeared to be the perfect compromise between someone who is caring yet confrontational, low key but direct. He gave me hope but made no promises. I knew after five minutes that I had found an excellent match.

Once I had decided in my own mind that this was the professional I could trust and who I believed could help me, I tried to figure out what about him seemed most significant. I liked his calmness. He listened very closely, and proved it by describing things I said in a way I had never considered before.

He asked me difficult questions that I could not answer. I liked that.

I think, above all else, I had an image in my mind of who could help me — and Dr. Wright fit the profile I was looking for. I enjoyed the messages I heard from him — that he would let me do whatever I wanted and be whoever I am. I realized also that it was not only important to be heard, but to be responded to.

It was frustrating to me that I could not put my finger on exactly what made this therapist right for me. He was not using any interventions or techniques that were not part of the repertoire of others. His approach also seemed to be somewhat similar to what I experienced before — an insight-oriented style that was part psychodynamic, part existential, and yet somewhat pragmatic. Yet, as hard as I could try, I could not (and cannot) put into words what Dr. Wright *did* that I found so helpful. Perhaps that was because it did not matter what he *did* as much as how he *was* with me. He seemed self-assured but quite modest and low key. He was intense but also relaxed. He was obviously quite bright but did not feel the need to prove anything. In short, Dr. Wright was what I wanted to be.

What was apparent to me was that he was a desirable model for me — in fact, he was the "me" I show to clients, although I rarely get a chance to observe that person. He was intriguing to me as a human being, someone I looked forward to spending time with. Yet as good as it felt to be with Dr. Wright, I still walked out of his office confused. For whichever therapist I stayed with, I felt that I would miss out on what the others could offer me — whether it was Dr. Genghis's bone-jarring confrontations or Dr. Glinda's soothing nurturance. Each of the three touched a part of me that was responsive to what they were doing and being. And yet I felt comforted with the realization that I really could not make a mistake: any of the three could help me grow; it was just a question of which road I wished to take.

Understanding Our Common Language

In their research on how experienced therapists select their own helpers, Norcross, Strausser, and Faltus (1988) found that decisions were made primarily on the basis of professional competence, experience, and reputation, as well as personal qualities such as warmth, flexibility, and caring. Indeed, like the 500 therapists in their study, I did not particularly care about which theoretical orientation my therapist followed, as long as he or she was an expert at applying it and had the capacity to treat me with kindness, compassion, and respect.

Also evident in my experiences in search of a therapist are the major themes explored in this book: (1) there are many different ways to be helpful to people, (2) there are some things that all effective therapists do, and (3) it is possible to identify common therapeutic principles and integrate them into a personally evolved style of practice.

What makes this task of searching for common denominators among diverse theoretical systems so difficult is the existence of so many distinct languages that are spoken among tribal groups: "If the phenomenologist uses terms like 'the phenomenal sense of self,' the psychoanalyst, 'projection of mental representations onto others,' and the behaviorist, 'conditioned stimuli and responses,' how are we to understand each other and develop a common framework?" (Messer, 1986, p. 385).

We have trouble communicating with one another when we speak different languages and come from different professions, training programs, philosophical positions, theoretical orientations, and work settings. And we have little tolerance for colleagues who operate differently than we do. What is truly amazing is that therapists who operate as differently as the three I consulted could all be effective with their clients. The inescapable conclusion is that we must have more in common with one another than we are willing to admit, including the definition of what constitutes a successful resolution of the client's presenting complaints.

Definitions of Effectiveness

What does it mean for a therapist to be effective? Certainly it is more than "having an effect," as the word implies, since effectiveness is judged principally on the basis of meeting stated goals. In the case of psychotherapy, we are also concerned with the kind of effect we initiate, since our influence can be for better or worse. Ineffective therapists may, in fact, produce more of an effect than those who are most helpful.

If positive outcomes are the criteria by which effectiveness is judged, then who determines whether the results are *positive,* and how is this decision made? If it is the therapist, as expert, who makes this determination when he or she has performed well, then the evaluation is subject to all of the biases and perceptual distortions that are part of any subjective assessment: "The client seems better to me, so I guess I've done good work."

Of course, we are actually a lot more obtuse than that. We will state essentially the same thing in progress notes, but cloaked in pseudoscientific jargon to lend credibility to our optimistic opinions: "There is a significant reduction in the frequency of depressive symptomology." This evaluation is usually based on two considerations: first, the observations of the client during interviews, which may or may not reflect actual functioning in the outside world; and second, the client's self-report about how much he or she has improved.

Ultimately, then, by direct or indirect means, the client decides the degree to which he or she has been helped. This is true for most other professions as well—it is the physician's patient, the attorney's client, the salesperson's customer who determines the degree to which the professional has been effective in getting the job done. The effective therapist, therefore, is a professional who produces a high number of "satisfied customers."

But this cannot be the whole picture. There are practitioners who, because of the way they work, are successful in their clients' eyes, but not necessarily in meeting initial treatment goals. They may be effective, essentially, in fostering dependencies in their therapeutic relationships, or creating distortions or denial of unresolved issues. One common way this takes place is in the assertion that: "You *are* better, you just don't know it yet."

Just as multiple measures of therapy outcomes (client self-report, observer ratings, changes in dependent variables) are used simultaneously in research settings, the clinician relies on several criteria to measure progress. While the most important is the client's assessment of "feeling better," we also collect data from family members, clinical observations, and a "felt sense" that things have improved. The compleat therapist is skilled not only in producing consistent positive outcomes, but in assessing all changes accurately and honestly.

Statistically Insignificant but Clinically Meaningful

Research efforts during the past three decades have been devoted to figuring out the complex puzzle of which core conditions of helping seem to be related to positive outcomes. Depending on which dependent variable is measured (client perception or observer ratings or frequency of behaviors), it can be found that variables such as empathy, warmth, and genuineness are important, are not important, or are sometimes important (Orlinsky and Howard, 1986). Based on empirical research, perhaps all we can conclude is that empathy may or may not help, but it does not seem to hurt.

Allen Bergin, coeditor of the classic research volume *Handbook of Psychotherapy and Behavior Change* (1986), laments his own frustration with trying to reconcile hundreds of discrepant studies and somehow integrate them into clinical practice. In an earlier work on the synthesis of therapeutic theory and research, Bergin (1980, p. 85) advises us to trust our intuition and personal judgment as well as the findings of empirical research: "The field of psychotherapy is made up of many different kinds of views and findings. With some we may have a fair degree of confidence, with some we may feel the data point us in one direction, but just slightly, and in others we may have to conclude that in the absence of data we are proceeding on what appear to be reasonable or warranted hypotheses or assumptions. Final answers are simply not available, and we must proceed on what appears to be the soundest path possible. In some instances, we can have confidence that our procedures are based on reasonably sound empirical results. In others, we must trust our own judgment and intelligence, recognizing fully what we are doing and the bases for our decisions."

We are left with the realization that research to date has not always supported those variables that most of us believe constitute effective therapy. There are more than a dozen different studies that show that even the clinician's level of experience is not necessarily a predictor of effectiveness. But, of course, we *know* it is, if it is the kind of practice that truly qualifies as "experience" — that is, further exposure to new knowledge, situations, opportunities that are processed in a way that fosters growth. The other kind of "experience" measured in these studies is the kind in which the longer a therapist practices, the more cynical, lazy, and rigid he or she becomes.

This lack of consistent, empirical support that can be replicated in a variety of situations over time is what makes the debates over what works best in our profession so intense. There are studies available to substantiate or refute almost any claim one would like to make. The behaviorists have convincing evidence that psychoanalytic treatment is nothing but the haphazard application of such principles of reinforcement and extinction. The analysts can demonstrate that the behaviorists are only dealing with surface symptoms and not getting at the root of problems. The cognitive therapists can show dozens of studies substantiating their claims that all other clinicians are missing the key to change, as can almost any other school of thought.

It All Looks the Same to Me

A stranger to our culture would be quite puzzled by what all the fuss is about — this bickering about which therapeutic approach works best, the conflicts and arguments about what makes therapy most effective. After all, to even the most astute observer, things would seem very much the same in offices across the land. Look in on a therapist, *any* therapist, and we are likely to see two people sitting comfortably opposite one another. Basically, the room would be furnished just like any other of its kind — framed pieces of paper and colorful images on the wall, bookshelves, a desk, a few chairs and a couch, a file cabinet, and a phone. Usually a Kleenex box.

Perhaps this alien visitor would be a little surprised to discover that in a certain percentage of these offices that also cater to little people of our culture, there would also be some toys on the shelves. But, basically, the office of any therapist would look pretty much the same. And so would the procedures.

Our stranger would probably assume that all practitioners of this profession do the same things. He or she would notice, for instance, that the two participants appear to like one another, since they seem at ease, take turns talking, and show caring and respect for what the other has to say. In fact, the alien would be surprised to find that this is the one place he or she has visited where people seem to truly listen to one another. This is obvious because there are no interruptions or distractions. Everything is quite private and discreet. They even repeat what the other says occasionally, just to show they are paying attention. Further, each member of the partnership seems to be more important than the other in different ways. At first, the visitor would assume it is the one who owns the office who is most important — after all, she occupies the most comfortable chair and seems to be directing things, even when she is silent. But then, the observer would notice that the other one — the one who sometimes cries or displays intense emotional reactions — seems to be the more important of the two. He is the one who chooses what they talk about. It is almost as if the other one works for him, the way she communicates an attitude of "whatever *you* want." And strangely, she does this without appearing subservient or sacrificing her own power.

From these visits to therapists, the alien would have to conclude that, while there are some subtle differences in what they do — some talk a bit more or less, some seem more or less permissive — there are few substantial deviations (although at one strange place the alien saw the therapist molding members of the same family into frozen positions where they looked like statues pointing or leaning on one another). The one person, who seems to need help, walks in, introduces himself, and tells his story. The other one, offering such help, listens very closely, asks questions, and supports the person to do what he most wants. Sometimes she offers more direct interventions, explains things, reminds him of previous things that were said, even challenges him to consider other alternatives. But to this innocent alien, not concerned with detail or trained to detect subtlety, it all looks the same. A person feels lousy. He goes to talk to this professional about what is bothering him. And he leaves feeling better.

It is the premise of this book that not only could an innocent observer be unable to discern significant differences among most therapists who are effective, but trained experts have their difficulties as well. When we filter out the jargon and the superficial concepts, what we have left is a consensus of effective practice. If we do not get so caught up in which approach works best and concentrate instead on what universal and specific aspects of each approach work best, what we will have is the essence of effective therapy.

What's the Difference?

In 1980, Herink published an encyclopedia of psychotherapy approaches that contained more than 250 entries. If we consider that in the decade since this publication the trend toward the proliferation of different therapeutic modalities has continued, and if we consider that the editor missed many other theories that are out there, I am certain that the actual number of conceptual frameworks would run into the thousands. Perhaps it could even be said that for each practitioner of therapy there is a unique implicit theory of operation that is being applied, one that reflects the individual personality, values, interests, goals, training, and experience of each clinician.

Yet all these diverse approaches produce similar results: satisfied clients. Luborsky, Singer, and Luborsky (1975) conducted a comparative study of all major forms of therapy then in existence. They calculated "box scores" from each outcome study and tallied the results, concluding that all forms of therapy studied have demonstrated effectiveness, and no approach to therapy works better than any other. In an update of this study completed a decade later, Luborsky and others (1986) concluded that whatever differences do exist in various types of treatment, they have little to do with the theory that is applied and everything to do with who the individual therapist is.

If we assume that all of the hundreds of therapeutic methodologies now in existence continue to flourish because they are helpful with some people some of the time, we are left with the conclusion that: (1) it does not make much difference what approach is used, or (2) all of the approaches are doing essentially the same things.

Even though therapists may be doing different things in their sessions — interpreting dreams, role playing, reflecting feelings, disputing irrational beliefs, analyzing themes, reinforcing fully functioning behaviors, among thousands of other possible techniques — it is apparent that most seem to be getting the job done. What, then, do effective therapists have in common if not a shared theoretical base or body of interventions? If we assume the differences are more illusion than reality, or that they are tangential rather than truly substantive, then perhaps we are all doing essentially the same things with our clients.

Similarities and Differences

While the premise of this book is that effective therapists have more in common than would seem apparent from their espoused differences, it should also be mentioned that there are several factors that clearly differentiate helping styles. In a survey of attempts to measure differences in theoretical orientations, Sundland (1977) described several variables according to which therapists differ — for example, in terms of their activity levels (passive versus active), directiveness (guiding versus challenging), structure (spontaneous versus planned), control (permissive versus limit-setting), temporal focus (past versus present), nature of alliance (authoritarian versus egalitarian), dogma (rigid versus flexible), and content (cognition versus affect).

Therapists can vary in each of these dimensions and still be effective. They can work in a highly structured way or a style that is more intuitive and spontaneous. They can talk a little or a lot. However, in spite of these variances, most effective therapists have a lot in common. Consider, for example, the behavior of some of the leaders in our field.

In the second volume in this series (Kottler and Blau, 1989), several of the profession's most prominent therapists described their experiences with failure, and by so doing, also articulated what they believe does play the most significant role in therapy. The following commonalities of what works in therapy can be constructed from what does *not* work in the therapy of Arnold Lazarus, Albert Ellis, Clark Moustakas, Richard Fisch, James Bugental, and Gerald Corey:

1. understanding, accurately and fully, the nature of the client's presenting complaints
2. establishing a productive therapeutic alliance
3. exhibiting confidence in the methods employed
4. demonstrating flexibility when and where it is needed to alter plans to fit specific client needs
5. being aware of one's own limitations and countertransference reactions that may be impeding progress
6. employing specific interventions with a defensible rationale that can be articulated

This last area of prescribing specific strategies with different clients and presenting complaints has been seen by many, such as John Norcross and Arnold Lazarus, as the hallmark of effective practice. In an invited address at an American Psychological Association convention, Lazarus (1989) called many of the conclusions of meta-analysts — and of other writers who believe that generalized effects of therapy are what make the greatest difference — utter nonsense! Lazarus explains: "There are those who have said it's all in the relationship. If you've got a good, warm, empathic, loving relationship, the rest takes care of itself. And if that's the case, why the hell bother to collect doctorates, study, take courses, if being a nice human being is all that matters?"

Lazarus emphatically states that there are indeed very specific treatments of choice for specific problems — lithium carbonate for bipolar disorders, response prevention for compulsive disorders, sensate focus exercises for sexual dysfunctions, limit-setting for borderline personalities. He believes that all therapists, regardless of training and professional and theoretical affiliations, should be able to agree on the most optimal strategies to employ with problems such as these.

In spite of a possible reconciliation of viewpoints regarding situation specific treatment methodologies, there is one bone of contention between many theoreticians and clinicians: whether the client or therapist should assume primary responsibility for therapeutic gains. Whereas some practitioners believe that the client is the one who directs progress and movement in sessions, other therapists feel just as strongly that the therapist is the one in charge. What is so interesting is that both strategies seem to work.

I suppose this really is not so extraordinary when we consider that unique styles of practice are part of any profession. Athletes can perform at their peak by strategies that either emphasize regimented, disciplined hard work or a relaxed manner. Consider the performance of baseball players. Some especially successful hitters are able to attain their level of skill through endless practice, the scientific study of relevant principles, and other forms of single-minded determination. These "left-brained" professionals are not unlike those therapists who are highly effective in their structured styles. Yet other "right-brained" hitters or therapists are able to be just as effective by relying on intuition, a relaxed manner, and natural and trained reflexes. So what *is* operable is *not* which style is used; rather the common variable is that the practitioner has developed a unique style that feels personally comfortable. And, of course, anyone who invents a unique theory is going to be even more at ease practicing what has been custom designed to his or her own personality, values, and needs.

Yet, another reason why the various forms of therapy are all effective is not only because they do the same things, but because they do different things. Each system relies on distinct learning principles. These could include mechanisms of trial and error, experientially based processes, didactic instruction, modeling demonstrations, reinforcement principles, gestalt insights, classical conditioning, gradual learning curves, response discrimination, intuitive sensings, problem solving, or neurochemical information processing.

Since individuals have distinct preferences in terms of how they learn best, therapies that employ some concepts are going to be more useful to some people than to others. Those clients who work well with structure and concrete goals are going to naturally gravitate toward a therapist who can work well within those parameters. And others who prefer the realm of the intellectual or the experiential will search until they, too, can find a good match. And then, of course, there are those who can adapt quite well to almost any system. But the point is that there are many ways to accomplish the same things.

I am reminded of a furious debate that took place at a hearing of a state Board of Licensure in which a number of rule changes for practice had been proposed. One of these included adding a mandatory residency requirement in doctoral programs that would effectively eliminate many alternative schools that are geared to older students who cannot leave or relocate their families to complete their studies. A representative of one prestigious state university gave an impassioned and quite articulate speech about the necessity of continuous, ongoing supervision and classroom monitoring in the training of a therapist. He believed that such daily contact with peers and instructors is critically important in the development of good work habits. In fact, he could not conceive of training a therapist any other way, and found it absurd that someone could ever be licensed as a professional who had not spent prolonged time in residence at an institution.

A representative from one of the nonresidency programs then presented an equally compelling argument: "I understand that *you* learn best in a formal classroom setting, and perhaps even the students that *you* have worked with do well in lecture halls and seminar rooms. I, however, have much preferred concentrated periods of interaction with my peers and instructors, with time in between these meetings to study, read, and practice independently. So what you are saying is that students who learn differently than you do can't possibly learn to be competent therapists."

There have been endless arguments among the representatives of the various schools of thought as to which approach is the best. Both sides level this claim: "You are patently incorrect, whereas we have the market on truth cornered. If only you would do what we do so well, then your clients would make more real/rapid/lasting changes."

Several things are clear: (1) different therapists do apparently different things, and (2) except for adopting certain behaviors that are known to have deleterious effects, no matter what they do, their clients get better anyway. Whether the clinician is fond of listening or talking, supporting or confronting, reflecting or advising, clients will typically respond favorably if certain basic conditions are met. Empirical research cannot yet account for the paradoxical finding that therapists who do different things get similar results, so that there is something else going on that we cannot altogether explain.

Shared Themes in the Client's Journey

There is doubt in some circles as to whether anything the therapist does makes much of a difference in producing positive outcomes; rather, it is the client who is effective or ineffective, not the clinician. This nihilistic perspective was expressed by one psychiatrist who claimed to have strong reservations with regard to *any* therapist or therapy as being effective: "In my experience the person 'undergoing' therapy is the one who is doing the 'getting better' and hence *he* is the one being effective. I know that many clients object to accepting the credit for their improvement and they will insist that the therapy has made them better. I cannot blame them. It is expensive stuff. Also, if you refuse responsibility for your improvement you can always blame others or external circumstances if things do not go right in the future."

The perspective revealed by this clinician — that therapists are neither effective nor ineffective, it is their clients who are — is somewhat provocative. Yet, it is a shared theme in all therapies that the client is the one who does the changing based on his or her motivation.

Stiles, Shapiro, and Elliott (1986) contend that "there really are different ingredients in the different psychotherapies, although whether these are active ingredients or flavors and fillers remains to be established" (p. 166). The authors attempt to resolve the paradox by pointing out methodological problems inherent in comparative studies of outcome. While they mention that indeed common features shared by all therapists (such as warmth and communication of new perspectives) or therapies (such as the therapeutic relationship) might override differences in verbal technique, they also propose that perhaps it is not the therapist's behavior that matters much. Maybe it is the client who makes all the difference. Those who have positive and realistic expectations, who are trusting and disclosing, who have acute problems, no severe personality disturbances, and who are willing to accept responsibility for their growth, are going to do well in practically *any* form of therapy with almost *any* practitioner.

Even if this were so, effective practitioners are those who can nurture the right qualities in their clients. Even those clients who are poor risks because they have negative, unrealistic expectations, chronic problems, and avoidant styles can be helped to change them. It is just in the way this is done — through pushing, shoving, waiting, or guiding — that methodologies are different.

To return to the baseball metaphor: ninety percent of all professional players can hit a little white ball traveling at 90 miles per hour to a place where nobody else is standing between 25 and 30 percent of the time. To the untrained eye, they all appear to be doing the same thing: standing there swinging a stick. But to anyone who has studied this activity, there are vast differences in technique that are equally effective. One can hit from the left side, the right side, or both, and yet that makes little difference. People have different stances, grips, rituals, training routines, philosophies, and strategies — and they all work if certain basics are followed (lightning reflexes, upper body strength, adaptability, and so on).

All of these things could be said about compleat therapists. On the surface, it does appear as if we are doing different things. Yet a new student of our discipline would have as much trouble seeing these differences as would a first-time spectator at a baseball game: we all look like we are standing up there with a stick swinging away.

There are those who doubt that it is possible to find a common factor across all therapy. Yet it could be said that the struggle of all human lives comes down to a single story told again and again in our mythology. In his classic work on prevalent themes in folklore, Campbell (1968) traces the common threads found in various cultures since ancient times. These myths are constructed not as a pure art form, or as history or entertainment, but they all tell the same story. He sums up (1968, p. 3) that "whether we listen with aloof amusement to the dreamlike mumbo jumbo of some red-eyed witch doctor of the Congo, or read with cultivated rapture thin translations from the sonnets of the mystic Lao-tse; now and again crack the hard nutshell of an argument of Aquinas, or catch suddenly the shining meaning of a bizarre Eskimo fairy tale: it will be always the one, shape-shifting yet marvelously constant story that we find, together with a challengingly persistent suggestion of more remaining to be experienced that will ever be known or told."

No matter whether disguised as Apollo, Buddha, Oedipus, or the Frog King, the legends and myths across time have followed similar rites of passage: the hero stumbles on a magical world that contains great obstacles to be overcome. These struggles lead to the crossing of a threshold and the resolution of life's riddles.

This journey that is so prevalent in the myths and legends of all cultures is also a vivid description of what the client experiences while undertaking almost any therapeutic journey. Campbell identified the following stages:

Call to Adventure. By some surreptitious event or blunder, a chance encounter opens a window to a new, magical, ominous world.

Refusal of the Call. There is balking and reluctance to accept the invitation; fear and apprehension scream out warnings.

Supernatural Aid. For those who venture forward, the first encounter is with a guiding figure (fairy godmother, angel, helpful crone, Merlin, Hermes) who gives advice and amulets as protection against the forces of evil.

Crossing the Threshold. The hero enters the world of the unknown, the darkness of uncertainty. He or she steps beyond the portals of secure ground onto more precarious footing — one that holds a promise of rewards, but also of danger.

The Trials. For a while things look pretty bleak. The hero is stymied and frustrated by the obstacles that seem insurmountable; however, with perseverance and a tireless will, he or she confronts a series of tests. The hero is supported by a benign power that cannot be seen. He or she survives the ordeals, wiser, stronger, carrying the spoils of victory.

Refusal to Return. With the mission accomplished the hero is reluctant to leave the magic kingdom and the benevolent protector. Yet the hero is commissioned to return to the outside world to give back what he or she has taken or learned.

Rescue from Without. The return is not without dangers of its own. Often assistance is required from someone on the outside — either a loved one who is waiting or the prospect of a new relationship.

Master of Both Worlds. The hero attains the status of Master after being able to travel between the magical land and the world he or she now resides in — without letting one contaminate the other. "Even as a person casts off worn-out clothes and puts on others that are new, so the embodied Self casts off worn-out bodies and enters into others that are new. Weapons cut It not; fire burns It not; water wets It not; the wind does not wither It. This Self cannot be cut nor burnt nor wetted nor withered. Eternal, all-pervading, unchanging, immovable, the Self is the same forever" (*Bhagavad Gita,* quoted in Campbell, 1968, pp. 22–24).

If this journey sounds suspiciously familiar, it is because, according to Campbell, the usual initiation rites and transitional rituals have been replaced in our culture by the journey of psychotherapy. This is illustrated in the following example. Brenda enters the office after a crisis has precipitated panic attacks — she discovered her husband is having an affair *(Call to Adventure).* At first, she was reluctant to confront the issue; maybe if she left it well enough alone, the relationship would end on its own *(Refusal of the Call)*. But her symptoms only became worse, disrupting her sleep, her appetite, and the ways she related to her husband.

With considerable help from her therapist *(Supernatural Aid)*, Brenda begins to explore not only the dynamics of her marriage, but also the circumstances that permitted her to feel so vulnerable and helpless in other areas of her life *(Crossing the Threshold)*. She attempts to confront her husband, who denies any indiscretion, claiming it is all the result of her overactive imagination. Unwilling to live any longer with a relationship she now realizes has been empty and destructive for quite some time, Brenda decides to move out on her own *(The Trials)*. Much to her surprise, although she still feels generally anxious, the original debilitating symptoms of panic have now subsided. She feels resolved to continue her efforts at growing.

Yet Brenda has come to depend on her therapist for support and guidance *(Refusal to Return)*. How can she ever manage being really and truly alone? They begin to work on helping her to internalize what she has learned and to wean herself from this transitional dependency. She starts socializing with friends more often and even starts to date cautiously *(Rescue from Without)*. She experiments more and more with her sense of power and self-control. This increased confidence is most evident in her behavior in the singles group she has joined: she takes a more active role in helping others beginning the struggles that she is now completing *(Master of Both Worlds)*.

The shared themes of mythological tales and the psychotherapy process highlight the universal variables that have been part of adventures in growth for thousands of years. While all compleat therapists (or story tellers) may not *do* the same things the same ways, they certainly deal with similar themes: confusion, frustration, anger, meaninglessness, loneliness and alienation, powerlessness, helplessness, and fear and dread.

Toward a Consensus

In 1985 the first "Evolution of Psychotherapy" conference was held; two dozen of the world's most prominent therapists were

invited to present their views and respond to others' ideas. The
stated mission of this auspicious event was to build on one
another's work and integrate commonalities among the various
ideas. These were, after all, the most brilliant minds in our
profession; surely they could devote their energies toward finding
common ground.

In reviewing a dialogue between object relations theorist
James Masterson and family therapist Jay Haley at this conference, we are witness to an event that has become so common in our field: the skewing of one person's ideas in an effort
to elevate one's own approach.

Masterson begins with the presentation of his ideas about how
the developmental object relations approach evolved. Haley comments that (1) these ideas have died long ago; (2) the phenomena
that were discussed do not exist; (3) Masterson's observations
are cloudy and ill-formed; (4) his attitude is so rigid and fixed
that he cannot see what is *really* going on; and (5) Haley's own
ideas make a lot more sense.

Masterson retorts to Haley that (1) he is wrong; (2) he is not
reflective and thoughtful; (3) he is so negative, rigid, and fixed
that he cannot open his mind to other possibilities; (4) he mis-
understands Masterson and his ideas; (5) his ideas are better
than Haley's.

If we were listening to children on a playground, this would
sound comical. But we are not. These are two of the brightest
minds in the field arguing about who has cornered the truth.
Neither will budge from his position. And we have heard the
same kinds of conflicting claims in thousands of similar debates
over the decades.

Now, I have always found this tremendously puzzling—that
is, why do Masterson's clients improve while he is working with
their individual dynamics of separation-individuation, and yet
Haley's clients also improve when he is realigning their family
hierarchies? And if this is not confusing enough, then how do
we account for Rogers's effectiveness when he is empathetically
resonating with his clients, or Ellis's successes by confronting
irrational beliefs? There are, of course, many other variations
that are equally effective.

In his analysis of the trends that emerged during an "Evolution of Psychotherapy" conference, Zeig (1986) concluded that once upon a time, all of the therapists in attendance were considered mavericks, considerably out of the mainstream in their thinking. As such, they were forced to limit their focus in attempts to protect their provocative ideas from attack. Now, however, their theories *are* the mainstream — and their proselytyzing seems to reflect rigidity and an extreme commitment to their own perspectives. Zeig sees little chance there will be much convergence among the different therapeutic approaches; he finds the authors of the various theories to be too stubborn, too committed to perpetuating their own ideas, too territorial in their thinking, to be open to greater cross-fertilization.

This, I think, is a tragedy. It is time to stop fighting among ourselves about which theory works best and about which of us really understands the true nature of reality. To gain greater respectability, efficiency, and efficacy, we would be much better off if we took the advice we give our clients: Let go of rigid beliefs that keep us from growing. Stay open to new possibilities. Create an individually designed set of values, but one that fits with what others are doing. Unify our experiences. Synthesize what we know and understand into ideas we can use. Integrate the past with the present and future, the person we are with the person we would like to be. Confront the paradoxes and polarities of life and resolve them by creating a whole being greater than the sum of its parts.

The compleat therapist is, most of all, someone who takes his or her own advice.

CHAPTER TWO

The Struggle to Find Things Therapists Can Agree On

One would think that the fellowship of professional therapists would be a fairly cohesive group, unified in the promotion of services and mutually supportive of one another's efforts. But this could not be further from the truth. It is the nature of our species to be territorial, to stake out our boundaries of private space with fences and other demarcations of ownership. This is true not only with our land, but with our ideas. Since the beginning of recorded history, we have evidence that wars over competing ideologies, religions, or life-styles are a "natural" way of life for human beings. And these battles go way beyond racial, ethnic, or national boundaries.

The tribal wars between competing schools of therapy are vicious, but rather than throwing spears at one another, we seek to discredit our adversaries through more subtle means. Sit in on the staff meeting of a large clinic and watch everyone go at it — the psychiatrists versus the psychologists versus the social workers versus the counselors versus the psychiatric nurses, each group believing they are truly just and do things the way they are intended to be done. Then, the ideological armies come into play, all fighting for dominance and control: The psychoanalysts ridicule the others for their lack of depth; the behaviorists mount their attack, accusing the rest of ignoring the most salient features of client change. The humanistic group sits patiently, planning their own ambush by reflecting the feelings of anger and superiority among their brethren, all the while feeling smug that *they* really know what is going on. And these "global powers" are all attacked by the upstart groups, the other 100 tribes who believe they have found what everyone else has missed.

In a cynical and humorous parody of therapists' tendencies to be "groupies" of a particular theoretician in vogue, Chamberlain (1989) offers a step-by-step blueprint for how to be the perfect disciple of Milton Erickson. She provides this advice because Erickson represents one of the few schools of thought that still has openings for apostles (this is explained by the fact that he did not write much himself, and that his work is so complex that nobody really understands what he did). In order to be a good Ericksonian, it is suggested that a disciple do the following:

1. Wear lots of purple (that was Milton's favorite color).
2. Know at least one basic metaphor (it does not have to make sense — sometimes it is better if it does not).
3. Take vacations in Phoenix (visit all the places Milton used to hang out; wear lots of purple).
4. Report a significant life-changing experience as a result of your contact with Erickson (since he died in 1980, you are allowed to include the impact of his videotape).
5. Get the jargon down pat (especially useful are *induction, trance,* and *intercontextural cues*) so as to sound as much like Erickson as possible.

This satire could, of course, be applied to any orthodox approach currently in practice. Psychoanalysis, behavior therapy, gestalt, humanistic, rational-emotive, ego psychology, or strategic family therapy all have their own disciples who pay homage to their creators, honor their memories, and flock together for mutual support. While providing a degree of comfort to us in affiliating with a particular tribe, the result of this "theory worship" is the proliferation of competing schools all vying for power, control, and a chance to be anointed the true heir to truth.

When Less Is More

In Kuhn's (1962) classic work on the evolution of scientific disciplines, he describes a state of existence in which there is no single generally accepted view about the nature of a phenomenon. For example, before Newton and his colleagues in the seventeenth century, there were dozens of competing theories about the nature of light, each of which made sense to experts at the time. It was Newton who was able to pull together these diverse schools of thought into a single organized paradigm with a set of established rules, standards, and directions for future research.

Pentony (1981) suggests that the preparadigmatic stage psychotherapy is currently in is remarkably similar to the chaos of competing schools of physics before the seventeenth century. He endorses Kuhn's observations on the development of science in general to the evolution of psychotherapy in particular — that is, that in the absence of a unifying paradigm, efforts should be directed toward developing one that will help to increase cooperation and decrease competition among scientists and practitioners. Continuing to gather more facts, generating more data, and proliferating more theories to explain the nature of human dysfunction and change only exacerbates the problem of having more concepts than we could ever deal with. As Pentony (1981, p. xiii) explains: "What is called for seems to involve a special kind of theorizing. 'Breakthroughs' in science seem to come from a way of thinking that penetrates into theory, reveals something of the assumptions that are involved in it, and in doing so opens alternative ways of contemplating the phenomena — ways which at first glance seem strange and unreal but which, when their implications are reached, seem obvious."

We do not need more theories of psychotherapy; we need fewer of them. We need unifying principles of helping that simplify the confusion of competing concepts, that describe the essence of effective psychotherapy and provide generally accepted principles that most clinicians could subscribe to. In fact, this movement has begun in the past decades, most notably by those such as Gregory Bateson and company, who sought to discover the underlying basis for human communication; by Carl Rogers, Robert Carkhuff, and colleagues, who have tried to describe the core conditions of helping; and finally, through the most recent efforts by dozens of writers and theoreticians who have been attempting to reduce the existing chaos.

There have been a number of systematic attempts to integrate diverse elements of effective psychotherapy into a unified system of helping. Some of these efforts are summed up here:

1. *Eclectic models.* Eclectic models are presented or critiqued by Woody (1971), Thorne (1973), Dyer and Vriend (1977), Garfield (1980), Palmer (1980), Goldfried (1982b), Beutler (1983), Hart (1983), Driscoll (1984), Held (1984), Prochaska and DiClemente (1984a), Fuhriman, Paul, and Burlingame (1986), Howard, Nance, and Myers (1986), Kanfer and Schefft (1988) and Egan (1990).

2. *Single theories that have synthesized attributes from a few other models.* For synthesizing theories, see French (1933), Kubie (1934), Dollard and Miller (1950), London (1964), Birk and Brinkley-Birk (1974), Kaplan (1974), Watzlawick, Weakland, and Fisch (1974), Bandler and Grinder (1975), Bandura (1977), Wachtel (1977), Lazarus (1981), Fensterheim and Glazer (1983), Murgatroyd and Apter (1986), Erskine and Moursand (1988), Kahn (1989), and Duncan, Parks, and Rusk (1990).

3. *Collections of research on what makes therapy effective.* Studies include Gurman and Razin (1977), Marmor and Woods (1980), Rice and Greenberg (1984), Garfield and Bergin (1986), Greenberg and Pinsof (1986), Kanfer and Goldstein (1986) and Norcross (1986).

4. *The non-specific major factor approach that seeks variables common to most methodologies.* On this approach, see Rosenzweig (1936), Hobbs (1962), Truax and Carkhuff (1967), Frank (1973), Strupp (1973), Marmor (1976), Cornsweet (1983), Karasu (1986), Omer (1987), Decker (1988), Mahrer (1989), and Patterson (1989).

5. *Recent integrative approaches to the treatment of specific problems.* To cite only a few examples, integrative approaches have been applied to *anorexia nervosa* (Steinlin and Weber, 1989), *bulimia nervosa* (Johnson and Connors, 1989), *the child molester* (Barnard, Fuller, Robbins, and Shaw, 1989), *self-mutilation* (Walsh and Rosen, 1988), *cocaine addiction* (Washton, 1989), *phobias* (Wolfe, 1989), *suicidal clients* (Bongar, Peterson, Harris, and Aissis, 1989), *borderline clients* (Kroll, 1988), *au-*

tistic children (Konstantareas, 1990), and *narcissistic disorders* (Gold, 1990).

It is in this tradition of unification, cooperation, simplification, and synthesis that the present work was undertaken. I am attempting to answer the question, What can we be reasonably sure makes an effective therapist?

The Advantages of Integration

The search for what makes therapists universally effective is growing. The majority of practitioners, in fact, are undertaking such a task independently — trying to sort out for themselves what colleagues are doing and why, and how new learnings from readings, workshops, conventions, informal discussions can be integrated into one's existing practice. Most clinicians are becoming more and more uncomfortable with the labels that identify them as disciples of any particular school, preferring instead the term *eclectic* to mean only that they are somewhat flexible.

In a survey of mental health practitioners representing four different professions, Jensen, Bergin, and Greaves (1990) confirmed previous studies that the vast majority of practitioners (68 percent) describe themselves as eclectic in their orientation. They also noted that among the 423 therapists in the national sample the trend seems to be moving toward integrative attempts between four divergent theories (psychodynamic-humanistic-cognitive-behavioral combinations, for example) rather than just combining those that are already closely aligned (cognitive and behavioral, for example).

It would appear, then, that one of the most significant challenges for contemporary clinicians is neither the mastery of therapeutic skills nor the learning of new interventions; it is the blending of what they know, understand, and can do into an integrated model of practice. Certainly, we are not very well prepared for such a task. Most of us were indoctrinated into particular schools of thought when we were young and impressionable. Our professors and mentors tried hard to influence our theoretical allegiances along lines compatible with their own — and they were largely successful (Sammons and Gravitz, 1990). We were not adequately instructed in the methods by which to pull together diverse points of view and conflicting ideas. Instead, we were after simplicity; things were complicated quite enough as they were — trying to stay in the good graces of our teachers, maintaining the approval of our supervisors, and not losing too many clients. Adventurism, creativity, bucking the system with too much flexibility might jeopardize our already vulnerable positions in the professional hierarchy. It was easier to follow the party line, that is, until we got out into the field and discovered that our clients did not care what theory we were using; they just wanted results.

In spite of the difficulties inherent in trying to reconcile conflicting opinions, divergent philosophies, sometimes even radically different assumptions regarding treatment goals, there are several reasons why the movement toward integration will only continue to flourish:

1. If we know what aspects of a therapist's behavior and being are most powerful and influential in promoting successful treatment outcomes, we can concentrate our efforts on refining skills and sorting out the specific ways in which they can be more optimally helpful. This can take place along the usual lines of trying to substantiate these assumptions through empirical research, as well as through the efforts of practitioners who can monitor their methods and those of their colleagues to observe common denominators.
2. There is increasing frustration and impatience with the bickering that has existed among theoreticians in the field for the past decades. Each proponent of a particular approach seeks to convince the world that his or her methods work better than any other. Too much energy has been invested in disputing the wrongness of what other professionals do, rather than in figuring out the rightness of what everyone seems to be doing.
3. It is somewhat embarrassing, when one thinks about it, to consider that the state of affairs in the therapy profession is such that there is so little agreement (at least publicly)

as to what constitutes effective therapy. The prospective client is faced with the task of choosing a helper among those who say it is best to address symptoms in a direct way, those who claim it is better still to examine unresolved conflicts in the past, those who favor attention to thinking processes or to affective states, those who say talking things out is most important, while others believe that being retrained, reconditioned, or reindoctrinated into new ways of behaving is most appropriate. The sum total of this chaos is that it does not seem like we really know why and how therapy works.

4.   There are mounting pressures from third-party reimbursement organizations to produce changes within certain time parameters. This has forced clinicians to be more adaptive in their approaches, doing some things with clients who have the inclination and resources to work in long-term treatment and doing other things with clients who are interested in different goals (Norcross, 1986).

5.   Integration means, for Mahrer (1989), reducing the number of theories in the field to a more manageable number in order to establish a common marketplace of specific operations and a shared vocabulary of terms with common meanings.

6.   It would be so much more useful in our teaching and supervising of beginning therapists to focus less on indoctrinating them into a specific system, and to concentrate more on the generic skills (such as empathic resonance) and attitudes (such as multicultural sensitivity) that most often make a difference. There are, however, many distinct advantages to affiliating with a particular theoretical approach, the most important of which is that it narrows the scope of our work to manageable limits; it is just too overwhelming to keep up with advances in all the different approaches and it is too impractical to maintain competency in all the various interventions. In other words, I am urging greater flexibility in our thinking and a greater willingness to adopt aspects of competing schools that we might find useful.

As convincing as these rationales are for creating a more integrative profession, there is also tremendous resistance, especially from those theoreticians who are vested in keeping their own approaches "pure" and undiluted by others' influence. In a volume devoted to the presentation of the dozen major systems of eclectic therapy, Dryden (1986) was stunned to discover that the contributors, who advocated so strongly a cross-fertilization of ideas, did not refer to, or draw on, each other's work! Even these eclectic theoreticians, who are committed to the integration of research, finding commonalities among diverse approaches, and following a pluralistic, flexible approach, did not particularly acknowledge the work of colleagues working along parallel courses.

Eclecticism, Pragmatism, Pluralism

The reduced influence of individual systems is due not only to the burgeoning number of new additions each year, or to the fierce debates that are waged between competing schools, but to skeptics within the ranks. Omer and London (1988) review three of the main approaches that are being slowly modified by their own proponents. Within psychoanalysis, for example, many clinicians no longer accept Freud's notions that it is possible to unearth "truth" from the client's memory or that the analyst should be a completely neutral figure. Among behavior therapists there is skepticism regarding the value of learning theory in explaining all behavioral phenomena or the appropriateness of dealing with only observed behaviors. And many cognitive therapists question the value of denying affective dimensions in favor of exclusively concentrating on cognitive processes.

The application of specific approaches has evolved into a new series of schools with different names and broader scopes: technical eclecticism, pluralism, pragmatism, nonspecific factors, microinvestigations, and treatment manuals are representative of the new diversity and synthesis. As Omer and London (1988, p. 178) explain: "Different responses to the systems' collapse chiefly reflect different assumptions of the systems' era: Eclecticism does away with technical purity; the nonspecific approach denies the importance of conceptual differences between systems; pluralism waives exclusivism in favor of relativism; microinvestigators dismiss the systems' units of analysis in favor of smaller and more common units; and the advocates of therapy manuals renounce therapy training by total commitment and lengthy immersion. The resulting changes, while profound, are *evolutionary,* not *revolutionary.* The new clinical and research psychotherapy enterprise which may arise from the present diversity seems likely, if anything, to be that of a maturing scientifically based art rather than of an ideologically based secretarian mission."

We have a number of labels describing methodologies of integration that are similar and yet quite different. The general term *eclectic* denotes the "process of selecting concepts, methods, and strategies from a variety of current theories which work" (Brammer and Shostrum, 1982, p. 35). Eclecticism has been further demarcated to allow for variations on this theme. For example, *theoretical eclecticism,* or the integration of diverse philosophies, is often distinguished from *technical eclecticism.* Eysenck (1970, p. 145) called the former "a mishmash of theories, a huggermugger of procedures, a gallimaufry of therapies, and a charivari of activities having no proper rationale, and incapable of being tested or evaluated," while Lazarus (1986) believes the latter is truly a systematic, empirically based methodology that employs a variety of techniques within a theoretical structure. Thus, Lazarus (1986, p. 67) says, "technical eclecticism sidesteps the syncretistic muddles that arise when attempting to blend divergent models into a super-organizing theory."

Unfortunately, the inconsistent labels and language among those interested in reconciling diverse therapeutic systems contributes even more to the confusion. Norcross and Napolitano (1986) tried to pin down the label that nonaffiliated practitioners prefer in describing themselves. According to their survey, roughly half like *integrative,* one-third prefer *eclectic,* and the rest cannot decide. The authors then attempted to add more precision to the meanings of the two most common terms. Whereas *eclecticism* implies an emphasis on the technical, the divergent, and the practical, as well as selective application of interventions to particular situations, *integration* is more often associated with the theoretical, the convergent, and the blending and synthesis of various parts into a unified whole.

Whatever we are calling it — eclecticism (theoretical, atheo-

retical, or technical), pragmatism, or pluralism — we are referring to the therapist's personal integration of all he or she knows,
understands, and can do into a unified theory that is adaptable
to change and evolution through experience. Prochaska (1984),
for example, finds an erroneous dualism between the search for
common factors *versus* prescriptive eclecticism. He points out that
therapists can operationalize the factors common to all systems
and *also* adapt their interventions to specific clients and situations.

Millon (1988) has observed that psychotherapists, like the ancient Hebrews, have wandered for forty years searching for a
common homeland and an integrated god. Yet it was only after being offered the guidance of the Ten Commandments that
the wandering Jews were successful. It is in this spirit of integration that Millon assumed the mantle of Moses to offer those commandments he feels are necessary so that a unified reconciliation between approaches can occur.

True integration is more than eclecticism, pluralism, pragmatism, or any other buzzword; it is the sincere effort to synthesize all that is known into a body of knowledge that is inclu-
sive, empirically and intuitively derived, and in which the whole
is greater than the collection of its parts. Integrative therapy
is much more than an accumulation of techniques or a merging of a few theories: it is nothing less than the synthesis of
philosophy and science, empiricism and phenomenology, research and practice. Millon (1988, p. 211) believes that the conceptual basis for treatments should be no less complex than the
concerns of our clients:

> The personality problems our patients bring to us
> are an inextricably linked nexus of behaviors, cog-
> nitions, intrapsychic processes, and so on. They
> flow through a tangle of feedback loops and seri-
> ally unfolding concatenations that emerge at differ-
> ent times in dynamic and changing configurations.
> And each component of these configurations has
> its role and significance altered by virtue of its place
> in these continually evolving constellations.
> In parallel form, so should integrative psycho-

therapy be conceived as a configuration of strategies and tactics in which each intervention technique is selected not only for its efficacy in resolving particular pathological features but also for its
contribution to the overall constellation of treatment
procedures of which it is but one.

This is an ambitious goal, but one that is well on its way to
being reached in a discipline such as medicine, which has existed a hundred times longer. In such an organized world,
therapists — like physicians — would agree philosophically on
basic assumptions of practice. Most doctors concur, for example, on diagnostic thinking, surgical procedures, standard office
practices, and even the mechanisms by which most diseases occur and are cured. That is not to say that they do not have
tremendous arguments, but these occur within a completely
different context from our own debates. While we are still concerned with the meaning and causes of symptomatology, medicine has turned its attention to the structure and mechanisms
of the body's immune system. Yet, we too are moving in that
direction of looking at the underlying processes of personal
growth and behavioral change.

The History of Therapeutic Integration

Trying to find the essence of what cures emotional suffering is
not just a recent trend. Over 2,000 years ago the first written
accounts of an integrative system of treating mental illness were
recorded. Hippocrates initiated the field of psychiatry by attempting to classify the various emotional disorders he observed
and suggested treating them with a unified mind-body approach.
He believed practitioners should be guided by reason and by
inductive methods of diagnosis, and he recognized the value of
dream interpretation.

In one representative example, Hippocrates treated King Per-
diccas II using an integrative form of psychotherapy we would
recognize even today. The king sought the services of the re-
nowned physician after all the court's doctors had been unable

to relieve his suffering. Hippocrates interviewed him for some time, gaining his trust. Eventually the king confessed that he was secretly in love with a concubine who belonged to his recently deceased father. Hippocrates believed that this intense longing was creating his patient's suffering and so diagnosed reactive melancholy. He treated the problem partly through dream interpretation and also by urging the king to acknowledge his feelings and to overcome the malaise of helplessness by acting on his convictions.

There was not much advance beyond Hippocrates' techniques until the last century or two. Until recently, a systematic treatise on healing was not considered a matter of great priority. However, some trends in earlier centuries paved the way for this development. The Renaissance brought with it many attempts to unify understandings in the search for solutions to human problems. Leonardo da Vinci combined science with art to understand human reality. Shakespeare created a literature of complex characters who manifested conflict and suffering. In the seventeenth century, Descartes attempted to resolve the dualism between body and mind. Other integrative attempts that followed—especially by Spinoza, Locke, Kierkegaard, and Darwin—set the stage for the birth of the mental health specialties. At the beginning of the twentieth century, Sigmund Freud, William James, and Emil Krapelin all worked independently to create a universal conception of human behavior.

When Freud and his collaborator Breuer stumbled onto the phenomenon that people feel better after talking out their problems, the profession of psychotherapy was born. A lifetime of experimentation and further refinement by Freud created the first comprehensive system of helping people with their emotional problems. Freud was drawn to the past, and this became the guiding force that led him to invent a method for excavating relics of the individual soul. Just as the archaeologist collects bits of pottery representing a past life, and then attempts to piece them together in an effort to reconstruct and understand a prior culture that evolved into our own, Freud sought to unearth the hidden secrets of the unconscious. His many pilgrimages to Athens and Rome were undertaken to satisfy his

insatiable curiosity about the historical heritage of culture. And
in his lifetime Freud spent a lot more time and energy studying
archaeology than he did neurology or psychiatry.

Yet Freud was only the first to integrate the diverse disciplines
of medicine, history, archaeology, literature, philosophy, and art
to forge the new discipline of psychotherapy. And at approximately the same time he was fighting his battles in Vienna to gain
respectability for his new "talking cure," William James was wag-
ing his own fight at Harvard for psychology as an independent
discipline that would combine both science and philosophy.

Dozens of practitioners who originally followed the tenets of
psychoanalysis — among them Fritz Perls, Eric Berne, Albert
Ellis, Carl Jung, Alfred Adler, and Carl Rogers — broke from
this camp to create their own schools. Of this group, Rogers
was probably the most successful at distilling the essence of what
empowers all therapy — the therapeutic alliance. He postulated
that the presence of qualities like genuineness, unconditional
positive regard, and empathy would lead to greater success in
sessions and improvement in clients.

Things, however, are not quite that simple. The search for
truth is an elusive enterprise, one in which we can never be sure
if we have the full picture. As the Russian novelist Turgenev
once explained to his compatriot Tolstoy: "The people who bind
themselves to systems are those who are unable to encompass
the whole truth and try to catch it by the tail; a system is like
the tail of truth, but truth is like a lizard; it leaves its tail in
your fingers and runs away knowing full well that it will grow
a new one in a twinkling" (Boorstin, 1983, p. 81).

In the 1960s many practitioners were convinced they had discovered the most effective way to do therapy by reflecting client
feelings and facilitating growth in the context of a nurturing environment. They were only to find that while their relatively
benign interventions did not hurt anybody, neither were they
tremendously helpful for those clients who required more active involvement in their sessions or attention to issues other
than their feelings. Also, many therapists abandoned the Rogerian method, or at least augmented it with something else, for
the same reason so many disciples of Freud abandoned psy-

choanalysis decades earlier: to satisfy the need to imprint their own influence on the therapy they were practicing. Thus Adler, Jung, Reich, and latter-day analysts developed their systems not only because they felt there was something else out there that could work better than what they were doing, but because they felt a personal need to follow their own path to the truth.

Is it narcissism and inflated ego that prevents us from following someone else's formulation of truth for very long and urges us to build our own monuments? Or rather is it that relentless human drive to never be satisfied with what we have, but to always strive for improved functioning and efficiency?

The ancient Egyptians were perfectly satisfied with their sun dial for measuring time, before the Greeks introduced their water clocks as a way to tell time even on cloudy days. And they too were content with their devices, although the English preferred their sandglasses, since water freezes in their colder climate. But it was the invention of the mechanical timepiece during the Middle Ages that made other instruments obsolete. The fifteenth-century monk must certainly have felt smug, now that his appointed prayer intervals could be clearly announced, yet several centuries later these primitive machines were in turn made obsolete by the invention of the pendulum. This brought portable clocks into being. And when the gear in these clocks was first created, people laughed at the primitive nature of swinging weights.

It is simply amazing to consider that until the last two decades we had assumed that the closest we would ever get to accurately measuring time is with a $2,000 chronometer. Now, for less than $10 we can find a digital watch that is accurate to within a few seconds a month. The lesson here is that each succeeding generation has been convinced they have finally found the ultimate truth. And just as we or our parents would have been truly astonished at the prospect that people would someday have video recorders and computers in their homes, what awaits the next generation?

Actually, the evolution of psychotherapy has been quite slow, relative to the changes in medicine during the past century. Many clinicians are essentially doing the same thing that Freud was doing a hundred years ago, with certain minor refinements. It was not until after the Second World War that writers such as Thorne (1950) attempted to integrate the concepts and methods of therapy then in practice. He was intrigued by the fact that so many different treatments could produce satisfying results and surmised only two possible explanations: either similar factors are operating in different approaches or there is more than one way to accomplish the same thing.

It is hardly an either/or proposition, since both hypotheses can be true. This was, in fact, the approach Truax and Carkhuff (1967) took in ferreting out what they believed were the variables common to all therapeutic systems. By examining the core elements originally proposed by Rogers (1942), Truax, Carkhuff, and their colleagues sought to identify those variables that are consistently effective in helping relationships. Accurate empathy, nonpossessive warmth, and genuineness became the watchwords for a generation of counselors and therapists who were trained according to a skill-development model. Thus microcounseling (Ivey, 1971), interpersonal process recall (Kagan and Schauble, 1969), and other skill-oriented programs became relatively atheoretical training approaches that stressed learning-specific behaviors practiced by all clinicians.

Current Efforts at Integration

Whereas the early twentieth century was devoted to the development of the first unified helping system, and the decades thereafter became a period of experimentation, the 1980s have been a period of rapprochement, convergence, and integration (Norcross, 1986). We have now reached a point where roughly half of all practicing therapists describe themselves as eclectic in orientation (Norcross and Prochaska, 1982). Never before has there been such flexibility and willingness on the part of clinicians to go to any lengths in order to increase their effectiveness. If that means abandoning exclusive allegiance to a single school of thought, so be it. Yet even those who function quite well within the parameters of a single helping model remain open to the contributions of competing approaches.

The International Academy of Eclectic Psychotherapists and the Society for the Exploration of Psychotherapy Integration were established to create a forum for the exchange of ideas regarding how divergent methods of treatment could best be reconciled. London (1986) has characterized himself and other members of these organizations as having several beliefs in common (although as feisty and independent a lot as they are, I suspect a number of them would object strongly to being classified with *anyone* else). These tendencies include a resentment of orthodoxy in any form, an attitude that is often seen by the major schools as antiscientific and uncivilized; a commitment to the scientific method of subjecting any methodology to public scrutiny; and the conviction that the nature of clinical work is so complex that it defies description in any simple language or single theory.

One of the most comprehensive attempts to integrate the best of all possible worlds is found in the work of Lazarus (1976, 1981, 1985), who merged the theory of behavior therapy and cognitive therapy as well as giving some attention to the affective, sensory, and interpersonal dimensions of human experience. This approach also recognizes that human beings are extraordinarily complex and multidimensional, requiring interventions that are adaptable enough to allow for vast individual differences.

Representative of the most recent attempts at theoretical integration is the work of Beitman, Goldfried, and Norcross (1989) and Norcross and Grencavage (1989). They undertake retrospective analyses of various approaches to create a framework that permits greatest flexibility. They attempt to reconcile the discrepant language used by various theorists (*catharsis* versus *self-disclosure* versus *presentation of data*); they also try to blend processes that are usually expressed as polarities — cognitive *or* affective, conscious *or* unconscious, insight *or* action, symptoms *or* causes, individual *or* family treatment. Further, they search for commonalities in clinical practice that are of pragmatic use and emphasize "goodness of fit" — that is, the match between certain client characteristics and presenting complaints on the one hand and specific approaches that are optimally effective on the other.

Current integrative efforts are therefore targeted more toward a prescriptive eclecticism for practitioners rather than a philosophical melding for theoreticians. London (1988, p. 4) contends that we are bumbling along into the same archaic metamorphosis that is usual for a relatively young discipline: "We are entering, I believe, an era of 'sloppy integration' in which psychotherapists will lack broad theories of personality for elegant systems of treatment, but will compensate for them with good *general* practice done by true eclectics and good *specialist* practice by specialists in problem-by-treatment interactions."

The voices of clinicians are finally being heard! London and colleagues such as James Prochaska, John Norcross, Arnold Lazarus, Larry Beutler, and others — are concentrating more on developing a framework for applying systematic application of therapeutic technology than on reconciling contradictory theoretical orientations. It is now recognized by many integrationist theorists and eclectic practitioners that even if we cannot identify common factors in all therapists, we can at least acknowledge that there are many different ways to be helpful to clients.

A typical argument for the pragmatic integration that now takes place in the thinking and practice of many therapists is presented by Corey (1990) who extracts aspects from each of seven different models to create his own unique approach. From psychoanalytic theory, Corey encourages his clients to talk about their earliest memories, interprets client reactions to him as manifestations of other significant relationships, connects present difficulties to events from the past, and recognizes unconscious motives. From existential theory, he helps clients to assume more responsibility for their lives, deals with issues related to fear of death, and interprets anxiety as a message to face one's freedom and choices. From client-centered theory, he uses himself and the therapeutic relationship as the major force for change, works on trust issues as a core area, and listens really intently, in a thoughtful, accepting, nonjudgmental manner. From gestalt theory, he challenges clients to deal with unfinished business, asks them to act out their polarities, and stays with his clients by focusing on the immediacy of their feelings. From transactional analysis theory, he explores early injunctions that led to scripted internal messages, identifies early decisions clients make about their conduct that are still operating, and accesses parent, adult, and child elements of client functioning. From behavioral theory, he uses rehearsal strategies to role-play behaviors, helps clients to set specific goals, and believes in the use of homework assignments between sessions as a way to facilitate change. Finally, from rational-emotive theory, he teaches clients they can change the way they feel by changing the way they think, challenges clients' irrational thought patterns, and encourages them to talk to themselves differently.

I would suspect that Corey's integration of these various elements into a personal eclectic style is not much different from the ways most of us operate. We are the sum total of all the teachers and mentors we have worked with, all the classes and workshops we have attended, and all the books we have read, movies we have watched, and experiences we have lived through.

In a review of the literature related to process and outcome variables in therapy, surveying over 1,100 studies, Orlinsky and Howard (1986) reiterate the conclusion that has by now become familiar: there is no consistent evidence that one treatment modality or approach produces better results than any other. This means that it makes little difference whether we are doing group versus individual versus family therapy, whether we are doing daily or weekly sessions, whether the treatment is time-limited or ongoing, or which one of the hundreds of theoretical models we are using.

If these are the things that are *not* important, then what *is*?

1. The therapist should feel comfortable with and have confidence in what he or she is doing.
2. A collaborative relationship should be established in which there is mutual respect, sharing, and bonding between the participants.
3. It is important to allow the client to talk, explore ideas and feelings, and experience emotional discharge.
4. The therapist needs to have an adequate level of competence in applying various skills and interventions that are believed to be helpful.
5. Mutual understanding and empathic resonance between participants that allows for risk taking and confrontation is essential.

Almost every effective therapist has integrated these factors into a personal theory of operations — whether it is a single mainstream approach or an eclectic model. Even those pragmatic clinicians who claim to follow no single theory or no fixed methodology nevertheless have organized their knowledge into some synthesizing structure that allows them to retrieve information, replicate interventions, and think through problems and conflicts (Decker, 1988). Most of these individually designed pragmatic models of practice, as well as the most orthodox systems, share several common variables that can be identified in the chapter that follows.

Chapter Three

Examining the Variables
That Are Common to Most Therapies

It is not that we do not have enough ideas about the best way to help people to change; we have too many. The prevailing movement in the field today is toward reconciling the differences between diverse approaches and finding their common factors. This trend has been shaped by several phenomena: (1) research findings indicating that a few core elements are at work, (2) a proliferation of eclectic points of view, and (3) sociopolitical pressures to develop a unified professional discipline (Goldfried, 1982b; Wogan and Norcross, 1985).

In spite of pressures both within and outside our profession to show a unified front, it is surprisingly difficult to find agreement about what effective therapy should be like. In a survey of therapists' beliefs about what constitutes good practices, there were only 2 items out of 83 in which there was agreement by more than 50 percent of respondents: that it is all right to break confidentiality if a client is homicidal, and that offering or accepting a handshake is appropriate (Pope, Tabachnick, and Keith-Spiegel, 1988). Although the focus of the study was on ethical rather than technical practices, it nevertheless points out the difficulty we have in coming to a consensus about anything.

A Consensus on Critical Moments

There is optimism for the future that we are getting closer to a consensus regarding what are "good" and "bad" moments

43

in therapy. Lazarus (1986, p. 167), believes that the hope in our profession lies in the integration of all the disciplines and theories into a technical eclecticism that draws on universal principles of what works consistently: "All effective therapists must straddle the fence between science and art. In a patient with bipolar affective disorder in a florid manic phase, psychopharmacologists have demonstrated that lithium carbonate, alone or combined with neuroleptics, is strongly indicated. The *art* consists of persuading the patient to comply with the medical prescription, as well as addressing intrapersonal factors or interpersonal networks that might require attention."

Indeed the scientific and artistic foundations for psychotherapy come together not in theoretical structures, but in a consensus of certain practices. In a survey of therapist beliefs about optimal professional practice, Mahoney, Norcross, Prochaska, and Missar (1989) found a convergence of perspectives. Although the 500 psychologists who participated in the study represented the full range of theoretical perspectives (approximately 25 percent psychoanalytic, 15 percent behavioral, 10 percent humanistic, 13 percent cognitive, 32 percent eclectic), there was some agreement about what interventions consistently facilitate client change. According to the participants, all effective therapists foster hope in their clients' expectations, provide support and encouragement, and clarify feelings, thoughts, issues, and themes.

As much as we might disagree with one another over philosophical issues, most therapists do follow customary procedures when confronted with certain specific situations. For example, the process for completing a mental status exam has become virtually standardized, as have assessment procedures for determining suicidal risk. Therapists of virtually all allegiances share a common belief in the utility of certain testing materials.

There are also certain events or moments in therapy that would be considered significant by almost all practitioners. They may be viewed as especially meaningful because of their relationship to successful outcomes, or because they are turning points in the direction that therapy takes. Usually there is some agreement between client and therapist that indeed something important has happened. It can be a "felt sense" that something has changed. There may also be behavioral evidence, characterized by increased intensity in vocal quality, accelerated activity, energy, expressiveness, and involvement (Rice and Wagstaff, 1967). These are magic moments. They are events in which things forever seem transformed.

From research and from many theoretical approaches, Mahrer and Nadler (1986) synthesized a list of "good moments" in therapy that are found in the work of most practitioners. These include the following themes, which are illustrated with representative client statements:

1. *Revealing significant material about self.* "I've never really told anyone before about the way my father would act when he got drunk. Even now, when my family gets together, we pretend like it never happened."
2. *Sharing personal and meaningful feelings.* "I know it doesn't make sense that I would be so devastated, but ever since I got the report about my low sperm count I just can't pull myself together. It means I'll never be able to have a part of me living in my child. It's so damn unfair after everything else I've been through! I feel so angry I could explode!"
3. *Exploring issues that have previously been warded off.* "When you pointed out a few weeks ago how self-obsessed I was, that I couldn't get out of my stuff long enough to appreciate anyone else's position, I felt hurt and misunderstood. But I think you are absolutely correct: I *have* been reluctant to look at how self-centered I am."
4. *Demonstrating a degree of insight into the meaning and implications of behavior.* "I've been blaming my parents for me being late to school—as if it's *their* job to wake me up every morning and get me ready. The truth is that I use them as an excuse for my troubles in a lot of areas we have been looking at. Yes, they fight a lot. Yes, they don't set limits with me the way they probably should. But it's my problem, and only I can do something about it."
5. *Being highly expressive and vibrant in communications.* "I can't *believe* he called me. ME! I *never* thought he even noticed

me. But he called—Can you believe it? This is *so* incredible! I just want to hug you, I feel so happy."
6. *Sharing strong positive feelings toward the therapist and the way things are progressing.* "You've helped me *so* much. I can finally stand up to people like never before. I don't feel like anyone can push me around anymore—not my kids, my ex-husband, or my boss. And yet you've helped me to retain the softness and sensitivity that is so important to me. I can't thank you enough."

As I read over this list of "good moments" in therapy, I feel a little wistful: they do not happen often enough. We wait weeks, sometimes months, before we see evidence of these signals that things are progressing. And for every good moment in therapy to which we could agree, there are also some perfectly awful moments as well—when silence drags on forever, when a client becomes abusive, when appointments are canceled without explanation.

If we can agree on which manifestations of client behavior are generally good or bad, the next task is to try to identify what is likely to facilitate desired goals. In a review of factors across all therapies that account for significant client progress, Lambert (1986) calculated the percentage of improvement that is a function of each variable. The most important single variable, accounting for 40 percent of significant growth, Lambert labeled "spontaneous remission." This includes all those factors that are part of the client's natural functioning, ego strength, developmental and homeostatic mechanisms, and social support. Another 15 percent of improvement results from placebo effects, which Lambert prefers to call "expectancy controls" because of their specific rather than nonspecific influence. So far, then, we have over half of generic psychotherapy's positive effects accounted for by client variables that are encouraged and facilitated by the clinician: expectations, resources, and developmental processes.

Once we get into the actual psychotherapy, about 30 percent of its effects are the result of common factors—such universal mechanisms as catharsis, empathy, trust, insight, modeling, warmth, and risk taking. Finally, only 15 percent of improvement is attributable to any specific interventions or techniques that are part of a particular treatment modality. This, therefore, helps to explain why the specifics of what we do seem less important than the more general principles we follow that are common to most therapeutic systems.

Karasu (1986) has conceptualized the specific techniques of different schools of therapy as belonging to one of three general change agents that are shared by all models:

Affective Experiencing. Whether it is called catharsis, emotional arousal, experiential activities, or the expression of feelings, all therapies deal with and process emotions. Behavior therapists would use flooding techniques. Psychoanalysts would use free association. Shared dialogue, role playing, bioenergetics, or any one of a hundred other techniques would also access the same material and accomplish similar goals: the identification, clarification, and expression of feelings.

Cognitive Mastery. There is also an intellectual insight component to most therapies in which clients explore the reasons and motives underlying their difficulties. There is great diversity, of course, in the way this area is addressed, with psychoanalysts using interpretation, behavior therapists preferring thought-stopping, existentialists exploring personal meaning, and cognitive therapists attacking the belief systems directly. Nevertheless, almost all therapists give some attention to what and how clients think about themselves and their life predicaments. Almost all therapies try to alter clients' perceptions of self and the world.

Behavioral Regulation. The third change agent is not within the exclusive province of behavior therapy alone. Any focus on behavior — giving direct feedback, identifying problem areas, selectively reinforcing desirable responses (even if they are only shared feelings) — are examples of how even a client-centered clinician would deal with behavioral dimensions.

These three general points of agreement among most effective therapists are only the beginning of what may be considered a consensus. The balance of this chapter is devoted to addressing more specifically many other factors that are common to the work of most effective therapists. While hardly an exhaustive treatment, this discussion does represent a summary of those factors that we can be reasonably sure most practitioners would agree are significant. These include supportive elements within the context of the therapeutic relationship, processes that lead to self-awareness and exploration, and variables that allow the therapist to influence the client's perceptions and behavior.

The Therapeutic Relationship

Of all the elements we might name, none receives more attention — both in theory and in practice — than the alliance between client and therapist. It is the glue that binds everything we do and the context for every intervention. A productive, open, and trusting relationship is, quite simply, the single most necessary prerequisite for effective psychotherapy (as we currently know and understand it) to take place.

The Relationship as the Basis for All Effective Therapy. The existential or humanistic therapist places primary emphasis on a relationship with the client that is supportive, authentic, nurturing, caring, accepting, trusting, and honest. All other types of clinicians — regardless of their espoused allegiances or belief systems — also spend some time developing a relationship that they consider to be necessary for anything else they might do. Most contemporary psychoanalysts, for example, no longer maintain the strict neutrality that was originally advocated by Freud, but rather seek to establish a more authentic encounter (Messer, 1988). And even those orthodox practitioners who do believe in maintaining a degree of distance so that transference feelings are not compromised still believe that *their* relationship with a client is central to the analytic work that follows.

Behavior and cognitive therapists will also now readily acknowledge that their interventions are likely to be more effective if implemented within the context of a relationship that is trusting and open (Wolpe and Lazarus, 1966; Goldfried and Davidson, 1976; Arnkoff, 1983; Linehan, 1988). I recall attending one of Albert Ellis's "road shows" during the 1970s and listening to his very strident presentation on the values of rational-emotive techniques while ridiculing Carl Rogers's emphasis on the therapeutic relationship, which he considered mostly a waste of time. He told us that therapy should be businesslike, direct, rational, and logical, concentrating on incisive confrontations of irrational beliefs.

When I volunteered to be a "client" for demonstration purposes, I discovered that although I felt better after my therapeutic experience, it was *not,* as Ellis promised, because of his rational-emotive interventions. What helped me more than anything in dealing with the impending death of my mother was Ellis's caring and warmth. Ellis — a caring and warm clinician? He had always seemed so cold and analytic to me from afar. But even before an audience of hundreds on a stage, I could feel that, for those few minutes, I was the most important person in the world to him. I could feel his support and his acceptance.

Yes, he quibbled about the language I was using to describe my plight. And yes, I did find his different perception of what I was experiencing helpful — but those techniques had a lot less impact than he thought they did. It was because I felt close to him, because I felt he cared about me, that I was motivated to listen to whatever he had to say to me, and I was willing to try thinking differently about my mother's death.

Qualities of Effective Therapeutic Relationships. The therapeutic relationship in rational-emotive, psychoanalytic, behavioral, or humanistic psychotherapy includes many of the same characteristics identified by Rogers (1957) in his influential paper on the subject — that is, a degree of acceptance, respect, and caring. From their review and analysis of the literature related to process variables that operate in therapy, Orlinsky and Howard (1986) further specified the qualities of the therapeutic bond between client and clinician. They found that the relationship is most helpful when it consists of the following: (1) an intense

investment of energy by both client and therapist that is unrelated to any specific techniques or activities employed; (2) a
reliance on roles in which the client demonstrates evidence of
self-expressive attachment to the therapist and the therapist
demonstrates an active collaboration in the process; (3) good
personal contact, including a degree of mutual comfort, mutual
trust, an absence of defensiveness, spontaneity, and reciprocal
understanding; (4) sufficient support and goodwill to permit
challenges and confrontation without jeopardizing the stability
of the relationship.

Orlinsky and Howard (1986, p. 336) summarize their findings
with the observation that the personal chemistry between therapy participants is not unlike the world of molecules — in which
some are attracted to one another, some are repelled, and some
form a bond, depending on their properties: "Our conception
of the therapeutic bond is intended to be analogous to a chemi-
cal bond. Some elements form very strong and stable combinations; others react with explosive energy; others do little more
than prevent each other from occupying the same space at the
same time."

Moustakas (1986) has described the essence of effective therapeutic relationships as consisting of three facets: Being In, Being
For, and Being With. The first process, *Being In,* is synonymous
with pure empathy: it is the experience of entering into another's
body and mind, knowing and feeling what is going on inside
the other. It is being open and responsive to whatever pours
forth from the client, with a complete absence of judgment,
evaluation, or analysis. It is the therapist's presence experienced
by the client as all-embracing and accepting.

Being For is, on the other hand, not a neutral posture — for
the client clearly feels the therapist's presence as an ally and advocate. With this support for him or her as a person, even if
not for a particularly dysfunctional aspect of self, the client feels
the impetus to pursue the arduous path that lies ahead, knowing there is an experienced guide along for the journey.

Being With encompasses the two previous processes, but involves recognition of the intrinsic separateness between two people. That is, while the therapist can try to understand, to enter

the client's world as a companion and promoter, he or she will always retain part of his or her own identity. It is client and therapist fully engaged with one another—sharing and exploring together—but sometimes seeing things quite differently. "Being With certainly means listening and hearing the other's feelings, thoughts, objectives, but it also means offering my own perceptions and views" (Moustakas, 1986, p. 102).

Reciprocal Bonds. In their evolutionary theory of psychotherapy, Glantz and Pearce (1989) have made the compelling argument that the reason why all therapy works is because it satisfies a basic need for human contact and engagement. We are a species of tribespeople who, for thousands of generations, clung together in bands—roaming the earth, camping out on the plains, living in caves, creating settlements. We are biologically equipped and naturally endowed to function in a world in which each person lives as part of his or her tribe, takes care of everyone else, and is in turn nurtured by all other members of the group.

Psychotherapy was born at precisely the time in human history when our tribes were disbanded, its members scattered across the globe. No longer do most people live where they were born, surrounded by their extended families and those who have been interconnected to their heritage. With these bonds disintegrated, with people separated from their kin, with families and tribes broken up through recent "inventions" of divorce, job relocation, and transportation that makes migration so easy, many, if not most people, hunger for closer affiliations to others.

The basis for all therapy is the establishment of a relationship that satisfies the client's need for nurturance, affiliation, and closeness to another. This is true not only for traditional individual psychotherapy but for the innumerable derivatives that evolved into various support groups. In the United States alone, each week over fifteen million people attend 500,000 different groups for alcoholics, overeaters, sexual addicts, abused children, disease sufferers, single parents, gamblers, women, men, and cross-dressers. "All of a sudden, people are pouring back into churches and synagogues with a fervor that hasn't been seen since the '50s. It appears that a great religious revival is sweeping the land — until you examine the situation a little more closely. Then you'll notice the biggest crowds today often arrive in midweek. And instead of filing into the pews, these people head for the basement, where they immediately sit down and begin talking about their deepest secrets, darkest fears and strangest cravings" (Leerhsen, 1990, p. 50).

In their essence, all support groups and forms of therapy create a surrogate environment that resembles the nurturing, supportive alliances of our heritage. They satisfy the millions of years of genetic programming that motivates us to survive based on the ability to form reciprocal bonds with others. Born without fangs, claws, or great speed or strength, humans have to rely on their wits and their sense of community. We are thus born with the intense drive to inspire trust and find it in others, even if, now separated from our tribes, we are doomed to frustration.

The great majority of clients, in addition to their presenting complaints, suffer from this need to connect with others. Once the supportive bond has been established between therapist and client, any number of different methodologies that follow are likely to be useful.

Self-Exploration Processes

Catharsis

When Freud and Breuer first collaborated in the 1890s on their new procedure called the *cathartic method,* little did they realize they were onto one of the greatest discoveries ever made about human nature. After Freud relinquished hypnosis in favor of his "talking cure," he learned that by simply allowing people to talk about what is disturbing them, they felt better after releasing repressed psychic energy.

Freud, as a neurologist, was fond of biological metaphors to explain psychological phenomena. Thus the notion of catharsis, or the release of psychic energy, comes from observations related to organic physics. Einstein pointed out that even inorganic matter is a form of radiant energy that is released as heat and light when there are small differences in mass (Zukav, 1979). Translated into human metabolic functioning, this means that the body maintains a precise energy balance. When energy input (food sources) is greater than energy output (exercise), body weight increases. The surplus energy available must be dissipated in some way, even if it is in the production of fat cells. This analogy of dissipating surplus emotional tension is the basis for understanding the cathartic process.

Now, all practitioners today may not agree with Freud's explanation for why catharsis processes work, but they would certainly not dispute the value of allowing clients to relate their stories with all associated pent-up memories, feelings, dreams, images, and ideas. Regardless of whether a practitioner believes in the existence of the unconscious, the libido, or the mechanisms of repression, there is, nevertheless, a fairly universal endorsement of allowing clients to express themselves freely, to share their feelings about their experiences and perceptions, to blow off steam, as it were. And apart from any other interventions that are employed — that is, despite what is actually done with the material elicited during catharsis — all therapies share the view that it is helpful to facilitate emotional release.

It is therefore a common strategy of most practitioners to encourage clients to tell their stories about how they got themselves into their present predicament. As a primary or secondary component of this process, clients are also stimulated to share their thoughts and feelings about what has occurred. And as a result, several things are likely to happen: (1) they experience emotional arousal, (2) they become aware of thoughts and feelings that were previously buried, (3) they feel better as a result of releasing tension, (4) if they are permitted to tell their story without detecting critical judgment in the listener, (5) they feel less shame and more self-acceptance about what transpired, and (6) they feel closer to the person they have confided in.

The value of catharsis is one of the few operative variables in therapy on which almost all of us can agree. Some clinicians use catharsis explicitly as the core of their work, facilitating the revelation of disguised as well as conscious material. Other therapists have enough respect for what this process can do not to

interfere with its natural progression in sessions. We all allow
our clients to talk, to speak whatever is on their minds without
fear of ridicule or condemnation. And we are thus all witnesses
to that magical transformation that takes place in which the
client, on unburdening himself or herself, walks out of our office
with a lighter step.

Consciousness Raising

Prochaska and DiClemente (1984b) identify consciousness raising as the most frequently applied process of change that is used
in some form by virtually every therapeutic system. That is,
the object of some part of the work is to increase the client's
level of awareness about some dimension, whether this is done
through feedback, guidance, or education. This information is
then internalized and used as an aid in generating insight,
facilitating decision making, or initiating action.

One psychologist feels that everything she does with clients—
focusing, structuring, interpreting, reflecting, confronting, even
establishing a therapeutic relationship—is done primarily to help
them expand their relationship with themselves. She describes
this phenomenon as it was played out with one client:

> Jan was twenty-four when I began working with
> her two-and-a-half years ago. She sought help for
> bulimia, which she had since high school, and was
> then actively engaged in binge-eating and laxative
> abuse. She also was struggling with male relation-
> ships and was attracted to men who would not meet
> her needs. She had tried to attend college unsuccess-
> fully while working as a physician's assistant. Jan
> was very frightened but willing to engage in an al-
> liance with me.
>
> In addition to fostering a safe and supportive
> relationship with Jan, I encouraged her to estab-
> lish a relationship with *herself*. I did this by assist-
> ing her to access her feelings and the well-preserved
> conflicts underlying her behavior. We spent time

exploring the impact of her father's early departure
and mother's desperate clinging to Jan and two
older sisters. We traveled into her self-image, her
sexuality, her "shadow," her spirituality, her experience of self, others, and life. At every step, I re-
mained with her in every sense of the word. As our
relationship has evolved, I have also disclosed more
of who I am.

Today Jan is free of bulimic symptoms, involved
in a warm, loving relationship with a man for over
a year, and just enrolled full time at a university
to pursue a degree in physical therapy. She attributes her evolving transformation to the journey we
embarked upon, a venture that called her to the self
she is still becoming.

The language and concepts that are part of this description
of consciousness raising are quite alien to the experience of many
therapists. Nevertheless, the same notion of introducing clients
to ideas that we believe are helpful to them, and increasing their
awareness of how they function in the world, is a fairly universal mode of operation. Certainly, not every therapist would agree
that raising a client's consciousness or promoting self-discovery
are sufficient conditions for change to occur, but there would
probably be little argument that it often helps facilitate progress
of the action stages. Clients will feel more motivated to initiate
changes in their lives if they understand how and why these
changes are helpful and what in themselves is sabotaging their
goals. Therefore, all but the most radical of Ericksonian practitioners (who echo Milton's sentiments that insight is distracting and even dangerous) will agree that some degree of self-
exploration is generally helpful.

Patterns of Influence

In addition to those aspects of generic therapy that are supportive and largely insight oriented, there are also a number
of factors that are designed specifically to influence the client's

self-perceptions and behavior. These include such things as impacting the client's expectations for treatment, creating healing rituals designed to heighten constructive beliefs, actively reinforcing self-enhancing actions, and facilitating tasks that are likely to produce desired objectives. Of special significance are those actions the therapist takes to promote greater self-acceptance.

Most therapies teach people to change what they do not like about themselves, and to accept what they are unable or unwilling to change. No matter what the client shares, what he has done, what he thinks or feels, he will still see the same impassive, all-knowing, all-loving face communicating total (or near total) acceptance. To the client who has just revealed he has evil thoughts, wicked fantasies, or has committed terrible acts, the therapist of almost any theoretical school will nevertheless respond in a calm, carefully neutral manner. The client may expect horror, outrage, scolding, disapproval, and disdain, and indeed it is possible the therapist may be feeling some of this internally, but what will show on the outside is utter serenity. No histrionics. No vomiting in revulsion, as the client may well have expected.

This unconditional acceptance has a profound effect on the client riddled with guilt, shame, and self-loathing: "If this person who seems pretty bright and together doesn't think what I said was a big deal, and believes I am a reasonably nice person, maybe I am all right after all." The experience of feeling accepted by another, no matter what one says or does, leads to being more accepting of oneself.

It is not a deliberate effort on the part of any therapist to initiate a plan of promoting self-acceptance in the client; it is quite simply one of the pleasant side effects that happens during the therapeutic hour. Long ago, we stopped arguing with one another about a few principles that have now become universally practiced. Prominent among these is the notion that it is highly desirable and generally helpful to listen with an open mind, to suspend judgment and criticism, and if not to unconditionally accept *everything* about the client, then at least to accept him or her unconditionally *as a person,* even if we may only conditionally accept certain aspects of the client's behavior.

Placebos and Positive Expectations

The essence of effective therapy is the clinician's unwavering belief in his or her capacity to promote healing and the ability to inspire this faith in others. Frank (1973), Fish (1973), and Pentony (1981) have all advocated that inspired positive expectancies are the primary ingredient in most change processes. To the extent that the therapist can help clients believe they are going to feel better and improve their lives as a result of staying in treatment, the more likely the results are going to be satisfying.

Internists often give relatively inert medications to their patients accompanied by confident predictions of how helpful they will be, and are not the least bit surprised to find that they worked just as they anticipated. Surgeons have also found that their patients tend to do much better if they are convinced the scheduled operation will indeed relieve their suffering. And all professionals realize their effectiveness is based, to a large extent, on their clients' positive expectations and trust in their competence.

A universal aspect of therapeutic practice is the establishment of a setting and aura that fosters belief in the process. All great practitioners exhibit an image of authority, wisdom, and confidence. They have decorated their offices carefully, adorning them with symbols of power (diplomas, licenses, a thronelike chair) and wisdom (books, manuals, file cabinets). They dress the part of the authoritative doctor or informal confidant, depending on the image that is believed to be most desirable. They appear at ease, comfortable, secure, as if they know exactly what they are doing. They act like they have been doing this for a long time and they are pretty good at it.

And the "it" doesn't matter much. Whether the interventions are medical, systems, or family oriented, or whether they are cognitively, behaviorally, or affectively based—if the therapist believes with all his or her heart they will work, and can convince the client they will work, then there is a great probability they will indeed be helpful.

In a major work summarizing the current research on placebo effects, White (1982) found that regardless of what medical procedure is used—surgery, medication, physical manipulation, or talking—55 percent of therapeutic effects can be attributable to suggestion. While once the placebo was conceived of as a distraction and nuisance, Wolberg (1986) states that if capitalizing on a person's belief system can have such a profound influence, much of what all professional helpers do is to promote the natural healing of the body and mind.

We send inspirational messages by both subtle and direct means—that whatever the client presents is nothing we have not seen before nor anything we cannot deal with. The fact that we are busy signals that others must be getting something from what we are doing. Our dress, style, and trappings all testify that we are qualified experts sanctioned by the state and profession. And perhaps more than any other single thing that we do that is helpful to clients, is that we believe in them and we believe in ourselves. We believe in the process of therapy. We are in the business of instilling hope.

Uses of Ritual

Every system of change makes use of rituals that are designed to attract and maintain the client's attention as well as to make the healing magic appear more powerful and impressive. Fish (1973) finds these rituals to be the basis for much of the placebo effect that maximizes positive expectations in all therapies. On an even grander scale, Campbell (1972, p. 43) has found that the function of all ritual "is to give form to human life, not in the way of a mere surface arrangement, but in depth." Based on his exhaustive study of mythology throughout the ages, Campbell believes that the use of ritual provides a needed structure to life, a symbol of order that repeats our most instructive themes.

The master of the Japanese tea ceremony uses ritual to perfect the harmony between the natural world and the human art form. Rites of passage for birth, death, marriage, or adolescence serve to ease the transition from one life stage to another. Rituals of religion, fertility, burial, or warfare provide a degree of comfort because of the power they have come to symbolize. The

hypnotist uses rituals to induce an altered state of consciousness that is more susceptible to influence and change. The behavioral therapist also uses certain operant rituals to reinforce
target behaviors. The technique of systematic desensitization,
for example, is an organized ritual in which clients list their
greatest fears, organize them in a hierarchy, and then face them
one at a time after undergoing other rituals of deep breathing
and relaxation training to induce an altered state.

There are rituals we use with every client to help them make
the transition from the outside world to the unique rules of interaction that operate inside our office. For instance, we begin
most sessions with certain inviolate rituals: the greeting at the
door, the walk down the corridor, the selection of seats, the invitation to begin. Similarly, there are rituals that guide the ways
we close our sessions, as well as those that facilitate transitions
from one subject to the next, or from one mode of operation
to the next.

Moustakas (1981, p. 24) describes the uses of rituals in his
work with children. In one case, he was especially struck by the
power of ritual as a way to make contact with an uncommunicative child:

> One of the most magnificent experiences I have ever
> had in therapy was with Barbara, diagnosed as
> schizophrenic. Since early childhood she had been
> humiliated, taunted, and called hunchback because
> of severe spinal curvature. My usual ways of be
> ginning therapy were ineffective. She sat quietly,
> silently, numb to nearly all of my interventions.
> One day she arrived looking weary and unhappy.
> She asked for a cup of tea. From this simple re
> quest a process of therapy was initiated which re
> sembled a Japanese tea ceremony—a series of rit
> uals each containing a special and unique meaning,
> beginning with the quiet preparations and culminat
> ing in the slow, savoring drinking of the tea. At
> these times, when Barbara spoke, her words were
> not edgy or agitated. She communicated different

aspects of her life and described her relations with
the people she encountered during the week. On
the whole she lived as a recluse, and rarely left her
home. Our weekly meetings became the pivotal
point of her life. In mysterious ways our rituals
awakened her and she began having regular contacts with others in her neighborhood.

Therapeutic rituals are designed, through their elegance and
symbolism and power, to facilitate an altered state of consciousness that helps the client to remain more receptive to the therapist's influence. The most basic of interventions involves simply persuading the client she or he really has no problem. When
this strategy is embedded in ritualistic patterns, such as adopting an authoritative manner and tone of voice the client has come
to associate with wisdom and expertise, influential effects are
multiplied.

A twenty-year-old man arrives at the office obviously distraught and embarrassed. He eventually sputters out that he
believes he may be gay, and since this realization, has been seriously considering suicide. When pressed as to how he arrived
at this conclusion, he told a story of having spent the night with
his girlfriend for the first time. Since both of them were vir-
gins, they consumed quite a bit of wine to appease their mutual
apprehension. When it came time to consummate the act, the
young man discovered to his horror that he was unable to maintain an erection. His girlfriend, who was also quite inexperienced
and insecure regarding her sexuality, became terribly frustrated
and went into a rage, accusing him of being a homosexual. On
three subsequent occasions he was also unable to become physically aroused.

The healing ritual became a simple matter of explaining that
alcohol inhibits sexual responsiveness and that failing to get an
erection occasionally was quite normal. He was then reassured
the problem would go away on its own if he would just relax —
which *it* did, after *he* did.

For this, or any intervention, to have much effect, it must
be couched within the context of the therapist's rituals. In the

previous example, the simple information and reassurance became immediately helpful because of the therapist's ability to create rituals that inspire trust and confidence so that the client would allow himself to be influenced by what he heard.

Learning Principles

All psychotherapy is an educational process that facilitates learning about self and others. Consistent with such models, therapy follows certain sound principles that operate consistently. Learning can be defined as any relatively enduring change in behavior that is not due to instinctual drives, natural growth and development, or temporary states induced by drugs or fatigue (Hilgard and Bower, 1975).

Reinforcement. If reinforcement is more broadly defined as support for some ideas and behaviors as preferable to others, then it is clearly a mechanism that is part of all therapeutic endeavors. The behavior therapist has in mind quite another idea, seeing reinforcement as the application of token economies, contingency contracting, punishment, or variable interval schedules to increase or decrease the frequency of target behaviors. However, Garfield (1980, p. 107) makes the interesting point that "the therapist tends to positively reinforce those responses on the part of the patient which he views as desirable, and to not actively reinforce or extinguish those responses which he deems to be undesirable in terms of therapeutic goals."

This concept is easily observed in the phenomenon that Freudian clients dream in Freudian symbols, Jungian clients dream in Jungian symbols, and behavioral clients report that their dreams do not have much significance at all. In another context, it may be readily observed that the client-centered therapist becomes more responsive (and therefore reinforcing) when clients share authentic feelings, the rational-emotive therapist deliberately and inadvertently reinforces the use of certain phrases and concepts, the psychoanalytic therapist gives selective attention to processes that are believed to be most significant, and so on. In short, when we like what clients are doing or saying, we let them know it. All "unconditional positive regard" means is that we should avoid the use of punishment when clients say things we do not want to hear.

Truax (1966) discovered, after analyzing Carl Rogers's behavior during interviews, that he was definitely more reinforcing of some client behaviors than other. Through the use of verbal acknowledgments and head nods, Rogers was quite effective in shaping the style in which the clients communicated, and even the content they focused on. This is true of all other therapies as well: we tend to reinforce clients, nonverbally and verbally, unconsciously and directly, when they use the concepts we have introduced, or act in ways we believe are more fully functioning than their previous maladaptive patterns.

Habituated Responses. In Seligman's (1975) model of learned helplessness or Dollard and Miller's (1950) notions of acquired neuroses, the assumption is made that clients have learned to be dysfunctional, and so it is possible to break these bad habits by learning alternative ways to think, feel, or act. Most therapies make use of the idea that fears, anxieties, and other symptomatic behaviors are adaptive in the sense that they are learned patterns of coping that have certain undesirable side effects (such as the present discomfort). It is usually proposed in some way that it is possible to act differently and to learn alternative responses that are more self-enhancing.

Acquiring New Information. Learning involves the input of new information that is useful to the organism. A component of each therapy system involves providing such knowledge when it is needed. This can take the form of providing general information about human nature (explaining a normal developmental stage of growth), about the process of psychotherapy (explaining the concepts of resistance or transference), about concepts relevant to the client's presenting complaint (telling a metaphorical tale), or other functions that are situation specific (offering guidance about where other information may be found). There is a part of every therapist's role in which he or she becomes a source of knowledge and information.

Transfer of Learning. Behavior becomes maladaptive when people attempt to generalize their actions from those few instances when it is functional to many other places where it is not. The client who is highly intellectual and analytic, who finds these talents useful to him in the financial arena, encounters only frustration when he tries to apply these skills in arguments with his wife when she does not feel acknowledged and heard. Much of marital therapy is necessarily pragmatic, because in order to break long-standing patterns of interaction, participants are encouraged to transfer their learning from sessions to their lives at home. This is also true for all helping approaches in which clinicians urge their clients to apply each week what they have learned in their therapeutic encounters.

Rehearsal. Most therapies contain some segment of rehearsal, in which clients are encouraged to practice new ways of thinking, talking, feeling, acting. They then receive some degree of feedback from their therapist that is likely to be helpful when they attempt to apply what they have learned to the outside world. This is not only true in the behavior therapies, but also in those that are exclusively insight oriented. Clients practice, at first tentatively, concepts and ideas they have recently understood to see if they are indeed valid. They may have just heard they are perceived as timid and so try to act more assertively in sessions. They have just examined an aspect of how they relate to authority figures (including the therapist) based on how they were treated by parents. They begin experimenting with more mature, less deferential communication styles. If they like the results they get while rehearsing with their therapist, they will hopefully apply what they have learned to other relationships.

Discrimination Training. Clients are often helped to distinguish between those behaviors that are helpful in one setting or situation, such as the world of commerce, but not necessarily in another, such as the world of love relationships. As part of the introspective process most therapies offer, some work is devoted to heightening awarenesses of when and how certain

patterns operate. Clients are thus taught to discriminate between:
(1) things they have done, thought, or felt in the past and things
they are experiencing in the present; (2) aspects of themselves
that are self-defeating versus those that are self-enhancing; and
(3) specific instances in which certain strategies are most likely
to be useful.

Task Facilitation

Apart from the learning principles just mentioned, there are also
many tasks that are usually completed in order for lasting change
to occur (Rice and Saperia, 1984). The therapist's job is to aid
the client along this path—by offering guidance, support, and
direction when and where they are needed. Some of the tasks that
are completed as part of the therapeutic process are illustrated
in the following case.

Andrew, at age thirty-nine, has been in therapy most of his
life. Although extremely bright, attractive, and personable, he
feels stuck and hopeless. He lives with his mother, who has enmeshed him in a web of dependence he has never been able to
work his way out of—even with the assistance of a half-dozen
different helpers in the last decade alone. His mother, too, has
been in therapy for quite some time. In fact, at one point, Andrew confided with a snicker, his mother was seeing three different therapists each week without any of them knowing about
the others' existence. "If my mother has all those therapists bam-
boozled, how am I ever going to escape her clutches?"

Each time Andrew would enroll in graduate school (he had
tried law school, medical school, and two chemistry programs)
or began a new job (numbering in the dozens), his mother would
sabotage his efforts by bribing him to come home. By now, he
was more than depressed; he was thoroughly *beaten*—without
any hope for the future.

His many therapists had attempted a number of reasonable
approaches over the years—and he had tremendous insight into
his mother's parasitic behavior as well as his own passive-depen-
dent tendencies. He could spout the jargon of psychodynamics,
existential philosophy, and a few other systems so well that it

took me a few weeks before I became convinced he was not a therapist himself (sent as a spy, I thought in a moment of paranoia, by some professional board to test my competence).

Here was a case when insight alone had not done the trick. Clearly, some sort of structure was needed to help him regain his confidence and hope by making steady progress toward some ultimate goal.

We started small. Very, very small. Since his dependency was maintained by the complete financial support he was receiving from his mother (each Monday morning he would find an envelope in the bathroom loaded with crisp bills), he began to withdraw a token amount to return to his mother with the cryptic note: "I don't need this much." Eventually, he was able to gradually increase the amount he returned, infinitesimally lessening his dependence.

We worked on task facilitation in a number of other areas as well. Since he was not at all ready to stick with a regular job, he served in a volunteer capacity that required a one-year commitment in writing. He contracted to attend a lecture series, moved on to taking a noncredit class, and finally actually began a graduate program. And all of this he kept a secret from his mother. By the time she did realize how independent he was becoming, he felt strong enough to neutralize her attempts (which by now he could easily identify as such) to sabotage him.

It is not usually my way to work in such a structured, task-oriented style. In Andrew's case, however, structure was *exactly* what he needed to improve his morale and sense of accomplishment.

There are other, more subtle tasks that are also included in most therapeutic processes — requesting clients to give vivid and complete descriptions of their problems, including antecedent events; asking clients to make connections between present concerns and associations with other life themes; and most important, helping clients to take risks by experimenting with new ways of thinking, feeling, and behaving. In fact, most therapies concentrate on creating a climate that is safe and secure enough for clients to experiment with alternative ways of functioning. Once freed of the fear of judgment and ridicule, once involved in a relationship with someone who is supportive, nurturing, and accepting, it feels safe to try doing things that may be awkward.

Therapy, almost by definition, implies the release of patterns that have been maladaptive in place of others that may be more fully functioning. The client initially enters treatment tentative, insecure, vulnerable, hesitant to take risks or try something new. Therapy often represents a last-ditch effort to get help when all else has failed. Like a battered child, the client flinches at the prospect of opening himself or herself up to more hurt, pain, and rejection. Only slowly, with the therapist encouraging and gently prodding, does the client start daring to be different. One step forward. And then wait to see what disaster lurks ahead. All seems clear. Another baby step. Still another. Until, finally, the client can walk, even run, without the need for further support.

More specifically, therapists are interested in helping clients to experiment with the following:

- When confronted with situations that you would usually avoid, face them with courage, and apply what we have been practicing together.
- When you catch yourself feeling self-inflicted misery, rather than wallowing in your suffering, *do* something to change the way you are reacting to what is happening around you.
- Whereas normally you would let this person or situation get to you, try something different, *anything* other than the way you typically react.
- Previously, you have viewed the events of your personal history as having limited you in the options you have for the future; the next time you will remind yourself there are other ways you can think about what you lived through, and thus other ways you can choose to act in the future.
- Ask yourself what you have been most strongly avoiding in your life — which conflict, confrontation, or unresolved issue — and force yourself to deal with it.
- You have been reluctant all your life to try anything that you cannot be perfect at, and so you have missed out on a lot of opportunities you could have enjoyed or profited

from. You will look for situations you can jump into, knowing you will feel inept in the beginning, but realizing that even if you do not live up to your expectations, you can still learn a lot.

We could, perhaps, list a hundred other injunctions by therapists that encourage greater risk taking and experimentation on the part of their clients. The objective of these efforts is to help people to stop doing things that they know will never work, when they feel too powerless or frightened to consider other options. We are all attempting to shake things up a bit.

Demolition Stage

After the Apollo astronauts had tried everything in their power to fix a million-dollar Hasselblad camera on the blink, an expert at Mission Control in Houston yelled out in exasperation to the ship circling the globe: "Kick the damn thing!" Which they did. And it promptly began to function. As therapists, we are also trying to help the client by "kicking the camera," that is, by shaking things up a bit so that things will fall together differently than they were before. We do this with every probing question we ask, every interpretation or confrontation we make. We are pushing the client to consider other alternatives, to expand the boundaries of what was considered possible.

Most therapies do, in fact, have what Schein (1973) called a "demolition stage," in which the client is first confronted with the fact that current life behaviors are not working very well. Clients begin to feel more and more confused and dissatisfied with present levels of functioning. They become more vulnerable in the therapy and are deliberately encouraged to do so. Dysfunctional character defenses are demolished through the persistent exploration by the therapist of the client's resistance, reluctance, passivity, and self-defeating behaviors.

When the demolition stage has been completed, the client truly believes, as he or she surveys the rubble around him, that it is futile to continue the previous course of action. The client may as well try something else.

Pentony (1981) believes that this demolition stage common to most therapies is necessary to prepare someone for lasting change. Once clients are at the point where they have given up previously maladaptive patterns that they now believe are useless, they are ripe for considering alternatives that include new perceptions of reality, new strategies for coping, new ways of thinking and interpreting one's life situation and what one can do about it.

How to Operationalize Commonalities in Clinical Practice

It is one thing to believe that there are certain variables and processes common to most therapeutic approaches; it is quite another, however, to apply these understandings to clinical practice. Let us assume, for example, that many of the elements mentioned in this chapter — notably the therapeutic relationship, the placebo effect, catharsis, and various learning principles — are in fact part of most helping systems. Further, let us assume that these variables are supported empirically by a number of studies attesting to their influence in promoting significant and lasting client changes. Operating pragmatically, then, what use is this knowledge for the practitioner?

Perhaps the greatest significance is that it helps us to focus our attention more clearly on which curative elements are most powerful, while filtering out those extraneous factors that are somewhat less important. Though only a casual football spectator, I heard a television commentator explain the dramatic improvement of a young quarterback's performance. Not unlike the work of a therapist in action, the quarterback must attend to a thousand different variables all at once — the positions of both his and opposing players, the time left on the clock, the wind direction, the playing surface, the history of what the teams have done before, what the opposition might be planning, what his own capabilities are, contingency plans, and so on. In addition, he has to memorize several hundred plays, or possible scenarios.

The commentator explained that once the coach decided to

simplify the playbook to less than a dozen options, the quarterback was able to relax more and concentrate instead on how he could improvise variations of these few plays according to his reading of the everchanging situations. I felt immense relief when I heard this explanation. It made instant sense to me that in my own work in therapy, I often feel overwhelmed by the number of "plays" that are available to me at any moment in time. I sometimes spend so much time analyzing the situation, sorting through options, and trying to remember what I am supposed to do in this situation that I miss a lot of what is going on. Like the quarterback with an overly complex playbook, I am so concerned with selecting the "right" choice that I am frozen into inaction.

I am then reminded of this metaphor: there are not really a thousand different plays, only a few good ones that go by different names. And I begin to ask myself silently: "What is it that *really* matters? Being with the client, listening hard. Being myself, as much as I can, without meeting my own needs. Letting the client know how I am processing what is happening. Reading accurately how the client is responding to my interventions. Just let the client be and do what he or she feels is right. Set limits when appropriate. Reinforce healthy behavior. Be supportive. Again. Be *really* supportive. Let him or her know how much I care."

With fewer but more consistent and potent "plays" at our disposal, therapy is more focused. Just as the young quarterback becomes seasoned and slowly adds more variations on the few themes he has mastered, so too can we expand our options. This quality—the ability to reduce complex situations to their essences—is only one of the many traits that are consistently found in the "compleat" therapist.

CHAPTER FOUR

What the Best Therapists
Are Like as People

Each of the elements that have been reviewed in the previous chapter are common to most therapies now in practice. However, there are also factors that transcend the theoretical basis of the various approaches and are found in the personality of the successful practitioner. These are qualities that constitute the essence of most effective therapists, wherever they work or however they prefer to operate.

While we may debate among ourselves whether such attributes are indeed universal, clients have little difficulty identifying what they most prefer in a therapist. "They are the attributes of a good parent and a decent human being who has a fair degree of understanding of himself and his interpersonal relations so that his own problems do not interfere, who is reasonably warm and empathic, not unduly hostile or destructive, and who has the talent, dedication, and compassion to work cooperatively with others" (Strupp, 1973, p. 2).

While personality style alone can hardly be considered the *only* operative force that facilitates client change, the qualities and temperament that a therapist demonstrates and models to clients make a strong impact on maintaining attention and influencing behavioral and perceptual changes. Whenever we think back on the people who made the most difference in our lives, immediately the images of several faces flash by. These were

70

people who were inspirational to us, not only because of the things they did to/for us, but also because of their dynamic charisma. This was certainly true throughout my own career as a client and student: initially, it was not ideas or theories that attracted me to a particular path; rather it was the influence of mentors I gravitated toward because they were like the person I wanted to be. In fact, like so many others in the field, I became a therapist to begin with because of the impact of a practitioner during my early life. I wanted so badly to be like her — to appear so together that not only could I help myself when I was in trouble, but I could even help others.

Modeling Effects of the Therapist's Personality

Clients want to grow up and be like their therapists. They want the serenity, the wisdom, the self-control, the confidence they see so effectively demonstrated before their eyes. They want to know what their therapists can understand, and they want to do what they see them do. They unconsciously adopt their therapist's speech patterns, mannerisms, and style. Their basic values change in a direction that more closely parallels those of their mentors.

Modeling effects are treated by most therapy systems in some form or another. Social learning theorists use modeling to promote vicarious learning processes. Behaviorists use modeling to reinforce imitative learning. Psychoanalysts capitalize on identification processes that occur as part of the positive transference. Cognitive therapists model specific methods of self-talk, just as existential therapists try to present those authentic qualities in themselves that they wish their clients to adopt.

If clients stay with any therapist for very long, they do so not only because they like the results they have seen in themselves, but because they like the clinician as a person as well. And the whole structure of therapy is designed to capitalize on these modeling effects.

In the classic "Gloria" film a young woman was interviewed the same day by Carl Rogers, Fritz Perls, and Albert Ellis to demonstrate their divergent approaches. And indeed there were marked differences in their styles, especially with regard to their operating premises, personalities, degree of directiveness, and type and frequency of verbalizations. Bergin (1980) felt confused by the relatively universal effectiveness of all three theoreticians and felt challenged to try and figure out some commonalities among their approaches. He noted that all three therapists did, in fact, share several significant ingredients. They were all acknowledged experts and authorities in the field, and therefore wielded a certain amount of influence in the eyes of the client. They were all passionately committed to their point of view and felt quite strongly that it was helpful. While all of them did somewhat different things, the client found each of them to be effective in his own unique way.

In a comparison between prominent psychoanalysts and behavior therapists, Sloane and others (1975) also found a surprising commonality among them. Their results were also consistent with Schön's (1983) observations that there is often a difference between espoused theories (what practitioners say they do) and theories in use (what practitioners actually do behind closed doors). In fact, what the researchers discovered was that clients perceived therapists of both groups as having similar qualities, and considered these same attributes to be necessary for successful therapy to take place. They saw effective therapists as: (1) having an attractive personality (something the psychoanalysts would deny is important), and (2) being helpful in facilitating some degree of self-understanding (something the behavior therapists would not consider important). In addition, they deemed it very important that a good therapist be an understanding person, be highly confident and skilled, and help them gradually to have more confidence in themselves.

On the basis of this and other studies that confirm the existence of universal therapeutic principles operating in all theories, Bergin (1980) stated that while therapists think the techniques they are using are all-important, their clients are much more concerned with their personal qualities. "Thus," he pointed out (1980, p. 140), "it is conceivable that many differently designated psychotherapies use many similar procedures or interactions which have an influence on the client, although they are either not emphasized or not attended to in the formal account of therapy."

Most effective therapists present an image of someone who is genuinely likable, who is safe and secure, and who is attractive and approachable: "The modeling performed by the effective psychotherapist, then, appears to involve, first and foremost, the steady presentation of a caring figure, whose positive regard will gradually be internalized by the self-critical patient; second, and simultaneously, the presentation of a strong, wise ('coping') figure, whose competent characteristics will be similarly internalized; and third, the transmission to the patient of a new value system helpful in dealing constructively with life problems" (Decker, 1988, p. 60).

The power of modeling effects thus helps to explain how it is possible that practitioners as diverse as Sigmund Freud and Fritz Perls could both be helpful to their clients. And if both of them were effective as therapists, it is not surprising that Ellis, Satir, Rogers, and Frankl can also be helpful, even though what they do seems so diametrically opposed. The question is, why do people get better when you reflect their feelings, but they also do so when you dispute their irrational beliefs, or interpret their dreams, or role-play unresolved conflicts, or reinforce certain behaviors, or reorganize family structures?

Clearly, the answer is not totally confined to what effective therapists *do,* but also involves who they *are.* The common thread running through the work of all great therapists is the force of their personalities and the power of their personas. They are the kinds of people who radiate positive energy. They are upbeat, enthusiastic, witty, and quick on their feet. They have good voices and are highly expressive in using them. Most of these highly successful practitioners are simply interesting and fun to be around. And they exhibit qualities that other people want for themselves.

The identification process is, of course, facilitated somewhat differently among the various therapeutic systems. Sometimes it is a planned intervention, such as a demonstration by the therapist of a particular behavior during a role play, or as part of a desensitization program. More often, modeling is simply a natural part of a learning relationship in which the client respects and admires the mentor. The client observes how assertive the behavior therapist is in stating positions clearly and unequivocally, and so experiments with being this way in his or her own world. The existential therapist discloses feelings about what it is like to be with the client, and so promotes greater openness on the part of the other. The rational-emotive therapist speaks in a deliberate manner avoiding the use of certain words (*should, must,* and so on) while choosing other phrases ("I made myself upset . . . ") and, lo and behold, the client begins doing the same thing. The Ericksonian hypnotist spins a metaphorical tale, and thereby helps the client to identify with the protagonist resolving a parallel struggle. Yet even apart from these specific applications of modeling principles, there is a more generalized identification process in which the client becomes more like the therapist in those dimensions he or she most admires.

The Fully Functioning Therapist

There is some empirical evidence (Luborsky and others, 1971; Garfield, 1980; Lambert, Shapiro, and Bergin, 1986) and certainly much intuitive reason to believe that the most effective therapists are likely to be those who are mentally healthy and skilled at resolving their own personal problems. This personal mastery is helpful not only in presenting oneself as a positive model for the client to emulate — a person who is confident, secure, and well grounded — but is also imperative in providing the basis for the self-restraint that is required during sessions.

It takes a tremendous amount of willpower for the therapist to avoid meeting his or her own needs or acting self-indulgently with clients. This could take the form of something relatively benign such as asking a question irrelevant to the client's welfare merely to satisfy one's own curiosity, or run the gamut to excessive self-disclosure, or even acting out inappropriate erotic, manipulative, or hostile impulses.

Self-control is required throughout every facet of the therapeutic encounter — monitoring behavior, sifting through and often censoring inappropriate thoughts, speaking concisely and to the point, and resisting the tendency to put the focus on one-self. And to exercise this self-discipline requires a high degree of emotional stability and personal effectiveness.

Because effective therapists are, first of all, effective human beings, they are able to function well in a variety of situations, demonstrating their ability to practice what they preach to others. In a classic statement on the importance of therapists being fully functioning human beings, Carkhuff and Berenson (1977, p. 272) present their credo: "In order to make demands of ourselves and subsequently of others, we must have ourselves 'together,' physically, emotionally, and intellectually. Functioning on any one of these dimensions is ultimately related to functioning on the others. At the highest levels, these dimensions are integrated in a fully functioning person, who is more than the sum of these dimensions. He or she is a full and moral being who is buttressed by a working cosmology that guides his or her development and directs his or her world. If he or she is not physically strong, he or she cannot protect his or her loved ones. If he or she is not emotionally sensitive, he or she cannot stand for what he or she believes. If he or she is not intellectually acute, he or she cannot advance his or her cause for the actualization of people's resources."

It has become increasingly clear to me that it hardly matters which theory is applied or which techniques are selected in making a therapy hour helpful. Effective practitioners represent every known therapeutic model. There is evidence supporting the efficacy of almost any set of interventions, techniques, and strategies — from hypnotherapy and bioenergetics to the most classical application of psychoanalysis.

It does not seem to matter as much as we think it does whether attention is devoted to presenting symptomatology or to underlying psychodynamics, whether the focus is on behavior, cognition, or affect, or whether the therapist talks a lot or a little. What *does* matter is who the therapist is as a human being — for what every successful healer has had since the beginning of time is charisma and power. He or she is perceived by others as inspirational and captivating. This is why "therapists" from the era of Hippocrates and Socrates to the most influential practitioners of the past century have all demonstrated their effectiveness by *apparently* doing different things. In fact, Freud, Jung, Adler, Sullivan, Reich, Lacan, Kohut, Ellis, Rogers, Perls, Wolpe, Lazarus, Berne, Frankl, May, Erickson, and Haley have all been doing essentially the same things — that is, being themselves and allowing the force and power of their personalities to guide what they do. All of the theorists invented styles that made it possible to play on their strengths. All of them felt restricted or dissatisfied by the methodologies they trained in and therefore adapted their methodologies to fit their own unique interests and values more closely. And this is true of all effective therapists. The furniture, the wardrobe, every facet of operation in a clinician's office is designed to provide a degree of comfort that allows him or her to be more fully himself or herself.

In spite of all the different personalities that are found among therapists, from the "histrionic" practitioner who is dramatic and exciting to the "compulsive" clinician who is methodical and perfectionistic, from those who are low key and easygoing to those who are highly active and verbal, there are, nevertheless, various attributes that most compleat therapists have in common. It is this "essence" of the helping personality that will be delineated in the following section.

The Impact of Personal Power

Perhaps more than any other single ingredient, it is power that gives force to the therapist's personality and gives weight to the words and gestures that emanate from it. It was the incredible power that radiated from the luminaries in our field that permitted them all to have such an impact on their clients, students, and colleagues. Nobody would have listened to them if not for their energy, excitement, and interesting characteristics that gave life to their ideas.

It is the ability to command and maintain a listener's attention that makes a therapist effective. And yet the hardest task of all for clinicians is to allow our unique personalities to show through without lapsing into narcissism, "showboating," exploitation, and self-indulgence. It is the quiet strength that clients gravitate toward, not the feeling of being overpowered by someone who must constantly remind others of what he or she knows and can do. So I am speaking here of a special blend of that kind of power that is benevolent and understated, coupled with a certain modesty and reticence in drawing attention to it. I am referring to power in the spiritual sense, as the kind described by Peck (1978, pp. 284–285) as that which "resides entirely within the individual and has nothing to do with the capacity to coerce others. . . . It is the capacity to make decisions with maximum awareness. It is consciousness."

Kohut (1971) speculated that it is the therapist's "religious fervor" and "inner saintliness" that exerts the strongest leverage in influencing others. Throughout history, the most powerful personalities were those who made the biggest impressions on others' lives. This is true of the greatest philosophers, such as Confucius, Plato, and St. Augustine; the greatest political thinkers, such as Lenin, Gandhi, and Jefferson; the greatest religious leaders, such as Mohammed, Jesus, and Moses; and the most prominent therapists.

Freud's impact on the development of psychotherapy was as much the result of his formidable persona as his cogent writings. Here was a man with limitless energy who eschewed sleep as a barrier to further productivity. He was the consummate communicator—passionate, convincing, brilliant in his use of the spoken or written word. He was a man of dignity and supreme confidence. And coupled with his many innovative ideas regarding the unconscious, dreams, sexuality, and human development was his ability to inspire loyalty in others. Rarely has an innovative thinker been able to attract a collection of disciples who were so brilliant in their own right. That Jung, Rank, Sachs, Abraham, Ferenczi, Adler, and even his own daughter Anna eventually moved on to follow their own visions is beside the point; they all drew their initial inspiration from Freud's example. And from exposure to Freud's charismatic power, his students and trainees were able to access the healing forces of their own personalities.

Power comes with the territory of being a therapist, whether we like it or not. In the eyes of clients, we are experts, gurus,

magicians. Yet as we teach clients how to do therapy for themselves, there is a gradual transfer of power. This process is
described as follows by a beginning therapist who was discovering for the first time just how this transformation takes place:

> The factor that "saved us" in the therapeutic rela-
> tionship was power. The client came to me with
> the intention of giving me her power. She had an
> array of various health professionals that she did
> this with. Since I was the most significant person
> in her life, she began reclaiming the pieces she had
> given the other professionals so that she could de-
> posit them all with me. And I found myself in a
> terrifyingly important position in this woman's life.
> Week after week she came, trying to pry my hands
> open so that I would grasp what she was offering.
> Each week, I would say, "No, thank you. My hands
> are full and yours seem to be doing fine, anyway."
>
> It was intriguing, and frightening, to be in a rela-
> tionship with someone who gave me all her power.
> I would watch myself in those crucial moments;
> time seemed to stand still as she waited to see what
> I would do. It was truly amazing to think that I
> could ask her to do *anything,* and she would readily
> comply. On one level, the part of me that has some-
> times felt so powerless, I reveled in this control; but
> at another level, I recoiled from this total power.
>
> I stood firm in containing our relationship to a
> therapeutic one. I deflected her "you-made-me's,"
> "you-saved-me's," "you-hurt-me's," and turned them
> back in her direction. We rode the storm of her
> anger at me because I wouldn't take responsibility
> for her. We worked until she understood that she
> could utilize me to work through her issues, but
> *I* was not her issue. And months later, she did un-
> derstand when I denied her complaint that I had
> caused her to have a terrible week because I had
> canceled a session. It was about two months later

that she finally realized that I would never agree to be responsible *for* her. She had arrived on the verge of a crisis, and asked me what she should do. I said "Change it!", and showed her the door.

Today, she feels exhilarated by her sense of being responsible for her own life. I shudder to think of how we might have become enmeshed if I had succumbed to the lure of the power she had so forcefully offered me. Reflecting on what happened with this client also makes it clear to me that, aside from the problem of the client's power being given to the therapist, there is the concomitant risk to the therapist of giving her own share of power away to the client. I learned it is our responsibility not only to help clients keep their power, but also for us keep our own as well.

Personal power offers the leverage for clients to believe in themselves, in their potential to counteract negative impulses, in their ability to change lifelong patterns of interaction. And it is this same power that gives therapists the opportunity and the capability to affect client perceptions and behavior.

Persuasion and Influence in the Therapeutic Encounter

In his seminal work on persuasion and therapy, Frank (1973) first postulated that throughout the ages, healers have been essentially professional influencers. The earliest therapists—from Stone Age healers who drilled holes in the skulls of the mentally afflicted to let demons escape, to the more scientific efforts of Hippocrates, through the various religious, mystical, educational, philosophical, and scientific practitioners until the present day—have all attempted to effect cures by persuading the client to give up some idea that was perceived as getting in the way, and to adopt another conception of reality that the healer believed would be more helpful.

Beutler (1983) views the therapist essentially as a "persuader" who is skilled at getting a client to adopt his or her own assumptions about the world. It is the therapist's job to convince the client to change maladaptive patterns, to adopt beliefs and attitudes that are potentially more productive. Frank points out that we are socially sanctioned and licensed by the state to persuade clients they would be more satisfied, not to mention more useful to society, if they would stop inflicting damage on themselves and others and adopt more constructive attitudes and behavior.

Most therapists would agree that clients would be better off if

- They understood more about themselves, their functioning and patterns, and their tendencies, fears, and goals.
- They stopped feeling helpless and sorry for themselves and instead took more responsibility for their lives.
- They were able to create greater intimacy in their lives and allow themselves to experience more love, affection, and sharing in their personal relationships.
- They stopped complaining about things they cannot control and focused their attention instead on what is within their power to change.
- They were not so anxious, frustrated, confused, and/or depressed, and they slept better and took better care of their health.

To this list could be added several more individual favorites of your own that are an implicit component of the assumptions you try to persuade your clients to consider for themselves. If psychotherapy is essentially a process of persuasion in which the client is encouraged to give up maladaptive attitudes in favor of others that are deemed more helpful, then the most effective therapists would be those who are most persuasive. That might explain how it happens that these very persuasive clinicians are so effective in convincing other therapists to subscribe to their models of interpersonal influence.

All therapists are certainly quite good at convincing their clients that they should let go of their symptoms and try something else instead. If we are not only effective therapists — that is, effective in our ability to be persuasive and influential — but also ethical professionals, then hopefully this "something else" we are asking the client to try is consistent with their own value system and not an attempt to create surrogate selves as an expression of our own narcissism.

All those who are potentially powerful — not only therapists but also politicians, writers, and many others — need to be extremely cautious about how this persuasive ability is used. Truly effective therapists are able to be influential in ways that allow their clients much freedom.

While we may assume that needless suffering is best relinquished, clients should be free to decide for themselves what is indeed "needless." Is guilt or grief or anxiety useless if it serves to help them work through pressing issues? It is the dialogue and mutual sharing that take place within the therapeutic relationship that allows the participants to think, influence, and be influenced in turn. For the clients are not the only ones who change as a result of this intimate encounter; therapists are profoundly affected as well by what clients bring to sessions. We are touched by their pain and suffering, our own unresolved issues are constantly probed, and we are also moved by our clients' joy and wonderment.

In this truly open encounter between people working so hard to be honest with one another, therapists learn to be even more persuasive by allowing themselves to be influenced by each and every client.

The Spark of Enthusiasm

One of the keys to therapeutic success is the ability to keep the client continuously engaged, involved, and connected to the process. The degree to which a therapist is able to elicit and maintain the client's motivation is directly related to his or her own level of enthusiasm. In the words of Beutler (1983, p. 28), "Judging from the impact of therapeutic 'enthusiasm,' it may be that 'If you are not enjoying therapy, you are doing it wrong.'"

This excitement for living in general, and for doing therapy in particular, is manifested in the clinician's voice, posture, manner, style, and presence. It could be said the object of any teacher is to stimulate interest in a given subject and then to allow the client's intrinsic curiosity and natural drive to grow to do most of the rest.

Compleat therapists are perceived by their clients as passionately committed to their profession. They are respected for their commitment to a life in service to others. Bugental (1978) believes the ideal therapist draws a sense of personal identity from his or her work: "I am not someone who 'does psychotherapy'; I am a psychotherapist." This identity is infused in our soul.

Therapists are also admired for the excitement they exude, the wonderment and insatiable curiosity they convey about the world, about people, and about what makes us the way we are. This enthusiasm is transmitted by the sense of drama in the stories we tell. It is communicated in the elation we can barely contain during a moment of stunning insight or shared connection. It is felt by the genuine caring we show, our intense desire to be helpful.

Like the best of the mystics and healers in previous centuries, compleat therapists feel a special sense of mission to banish suffering from the earth—or at least that corner of it that is under our influence. There is nothing more uplifting for a despondent, disillusioned, distraught human being to encounter than to walk into a room and find someone waiting who radiates light in a world of darkness. This enthusiasm and excitement in the therapist's manner becomes contagious. As if by transfusion, the client too becomes more animated and hopeful and enthusiastic about possibilities for the future.

The Value of Humor and Play

Enthusiasm, power, and influence all come together in the therapist's appreciation for and active use of humor. There are, of course, many effective therapists who are quite solemn and serious in their endeavors—so that it would not be quite fair or accurate to insist that being witty is a necessity in order to be helpful. But it usually helps.

Madanes (1986, p. 51) has said about the therapist's sense of humor: "What makes change possible is the therapist's ability to be optimistic and to see what is funny or appealing in a grim situation." Many other therapists share her belief that taking oneself too seriously is the cause, if not the primary factor, in most emotional suffering. The effective therapist can dilute the client's negativity, pessimism, and hopelessness by introducing a degree of playfulness to a depressing situation.

Bergman (1985, p. 184) comments on how he is able to stay vibrant and alive as a therapist: "When I am in a treatment session, I am, of course, focused on helping a family change, but I am also out to have some fun. Not only do I need to have fun and be playful, but sometimes, if I can get away with it, I also try to push the fun and play to joy. I'm doing this for me, but I suspect there are also clinical spin-offs that work therapeutically toward change."

Bergman goes on to describe the value of humor and play in therapy. Besides serving as entertainment and leading to the shared joy of laughter, humor and play can

- reduce tension and discharge energy
- lighten affect from despair and suffering
- provide intellectual stimulation
- contribute to creative thinking
- help keep things in perspective
- make it easier to deal with the incongruous, awkward, and nonsensical aspects in life
- make it possible to explore forbidden subjects in less threatening ways
- express exuberance and warmth
- create a bond between persons sharing a joke
- parody some aspect of behavior for greater awareness

The therapist's sense of humor, then, is a reflection of the joy, passion, creativity, and playfulness that are the hallmarks of any interesting character. It is what makes him or her appear less threatening and more approachable. It is what allows him or her to deal with intensely serious subjects over and over again and still to keep a sense of perspective.

Harper (1985) reports that having fun is one of his major goals in therapy. People take their suffering all too seriously and need to let go of their dreary perceptions and replace them with others that are more joyful. "I try to get some fun out of even basically tragic, onerous, tedious, and unpleasant situations in and out of therapy, and I try to pass on this approach to the people I see in my practice. . . . The central idea I model and teach is to take responsibilities seriously, but get whatever pleasure possible out of the process of so doing" (Harper, 1985, p. 10).

There are many anecdotes circulating around about the exploits of Milton Erickson, especially with regard to his creative use of humor and psychological shock in therapy to break repetitive dysfunctional patterns. One of these stories, related by Rossi (1973), describes a case presented by Erickson at a psychiatric conference. While few clinicians would ever dream of going to the extremes that Erickson (and the subsequent generation of directive strategic therapists) was willing to try in an effort to jar client defenses, the following case is an intriguing example of the therapist's creative potential.

A couple came to Erickson in considerable distress over their failure to have a baby, although there were no organic impediments and they had been trying for some time. The husband and wife appeared quite stilted, formal, and ill at ease, becoming even more so when trying to discuss their delicate problem. In their own distinctive style, the couple revealed their problem: "Because of our desire for children we have engaged in the marital union with full physiological concomitant each night and morning for procreative purposes. On Sundays and holidays we have engaged in the marital union with physiological concomitant for procreative purposes as much as four times a day. We have not permitted physical disability to interfere. As a result of the frustration of our philoprogenitive desires, the marital union has become progressively unpleasant for us but it has not interfered with our efforts at procreation; but it does distress both of us to discover our increasing impatience with each other. For this reason we are seeking your aid since other medical aid has failed" (Rossi, 1973, p. 10).

In view of Erickson's indomitable sense of humor, we can only imagine his amusement in listening to this presentation. We do know, however, what he did. After telling the couple that he might have a cure for their problem, he warned them it would involve a severe psychological shock. He then left them alone for fifteen minutes to decide whether they thought they could handle the proposed treatment that would be quite shocking.

On returning to the room, Erickson obtained their consent and then prepared them for the "event." He suggested they hang tightly to their chairs in anticipation of what he would say. He also asked that they refrain from talking to one another about what they were about to hear. They should remain perfectly silent until they were back in their own home. He then began: "For three long years you have engaged in the marital union with full physiological concomitant for procreative purposes at least twice a day and sometimes as much as four times in twenty-four hours, and you have met with defeat of your philoprogenitive drive. Now why in hell don't you fuck for fun and pray to the devil that she isn't knocked up for at least three months. Now please leave" (Rossi, 1973, p. 10).

Similar to so many of the Erickson legends, this one, too, had a happy ending. The couple was predictably shocked by what they heard (as were the members of the psychiatric conference, when the "F" word was used). Yet as soon as they arrived home they fell to the floor in a mad, passionate frolic. Within three months the wife became pregnant.

What is most instructive about Erickson's cases are not his often bizarre actions that most practitioners would have some difficulty employing, but rather his incredibly inventive, playful, and original way of thinking about client problems. Erickson became the prototype for the role of therapist as "wise fool," for as Gomez and O'Connell (1987, p. 43) have explained, fools are so internally free that "they can be masters of reconciling contraditions, and can incarnate a living sense of wonder." Effective therapists thus have the capacity to be tastefully and tactfully humorous in ways to disarm client resistance and help clients face painfully serious issues.

Caring and Warmth

In whatever form and style it is manifested, clients feel motivated to keep working on themselves when they feel there is someone in their corner who genuinely cares about them.

It does not matter how we show this caring—by being permissive and indulgent, or firm in our limit-setting. Whatever messages we choose to impart, and however we decide to work, as long as clients sense our commitment to them and feel our regard, they will show increased capacities for caring for themselves. The reasoning goes something like this: (1) "This person who is my therapist seems to me to be pretty knowledgeable, competent, and a good judge of character"; (2) "The therapist obviously likes me and genuinely believes I have a lot going for me"; (3) "If the therapist thinks I am a pretty nice person, and I trust this person's judgment, then I must have a lot more on the ball than I thought I did"; and (4) "I'd better start treating myself like my therapist believes I deserve to be treated."

A social worker who specializes in working with oppositional adolescents finds that whatever else he does—confrontation, behavior modification, role playing, school interventions—the way he shows his concern for his clients' welfare has the greatest impact. He describes how this operates in the case of one especially difficult child:

> A couple of years ago, I began working with a fifteen-year-old male who presented the following problems: (1) lying, (2) impulsive behavior, (3) poor academic functioning, and (4) antisocial behavior (car theft, skipping school, fighting, trafficking drugs). My work with this child was rather unsuccessful in that our contact was sporadic and a true relationship nonexistent.
>
> Due to continued acting out, he was placed in a detention facility, where I continued to see him. His first response to my continued involvement was one of shock, especially since we had never developed a relationship when I saw him in my office. He initially remained rather evasive and knew how to say the right things. On a leave from the program, he was involved in using a gun trying to frighten another person, after which he was returned with more serious charges. When I went back to

see him, the first change was his attitude toward me. Several times he made a point that I had not given up on him, giving him a sense of positive importance. He became more open regarding his past behaviors, relating them to anger and frustration due to past family experiences. As his parents became involved in treatment, communication improved with them; he became more willing to accept responsibility for his actions. Initially, the boy was only able to talk with me about his feelings regarding his parents, and the parents to me about their feelings toward their son. Eventually, they were brought together in family sessions and they got along quite well. He is now back at home and doing fine.

When I ask myself what happened with this boy, I really don't think it had much to do with my interventions. One clue was found on the envelope to a letter he wrote me. It was addressed to: "The Best Man on Earth." This boy, who had been pushed around his whole life, turned things around because there was one person in his world who really cared about him.

Guy (1987, p. 294) believes that what distinguishes the truly outstanding therapist from those who just go through the motions is something more than skill and expertise: "He or she possesses a deep sense of caring and compassion that results in a level of empathy and sensitivity that touches others in very extraordinary ways. . . . There is a resultant transcendence which enables these special individuals to accomplish the 'impossible thing'. . . . Whether in session or on vacation, the fully integrated therapist constantly shares his or her senses of perspective and worldview. A personal passion for psychic wholeness is incorporated into nearly every encounter, not because of an uncontrollable drive, but due to a genuine sense of mutuality and caring."

More than all the techniques and expertise, all the wisdom

and perceptiveness, being a genuinely nice person makes a therapist helpful. This is a human being who, for whatever reasons, is liked by others. It makes little difference which specific qualities are evident — whether he or she is a lovable, huggable figure, a crusty eccentric, or a somewhat controlled and restrained individual. If the therapist is perceived by clients as "nice," he or she is almost certainly going to be trusted, admired, and listened to.

Credibility and Confidence

Therapists who are perceived as confident and credible produce positive results. Period. And if they are viewed as being self-congruent and genuine, all the better (Orlinsky and Howard, 1986).

So what do therapists who have credibility and confidence look like, and how do they act? They are people at ease with themselves, natural in their gestures and movements — as if every part of them is an expression of an inner core that is satisfied and self-assured. They are comfortable in their bodies; with their words and nonverbal cues, they communicate that they know who they are, where they have been, and where they are going. Their sense of their own worth allows them to readily admit their confusions without losing any credibility. It is the ultimate in confidence to disclose that you do not know what is going on but feel reasonably certain that eventually you will find out.

Credible, confident therapists can back up their optimistic predictions and assurance with definite results. Anybody can pretend to know what he or she is doing, but the ultimate test is to deliver what has been implicitly promised. Credibility comes from doing what we said we would do — even if that is quite simply to listen. Good therapists convey the impression that:

- I like myself.
- And I like you, too.
- I know what I'm doing.
- I've done this many times before.
- I can help you.

If these are the promises that initially help therapists project confidence, they sustain their credibility by living up to the contract. When our interpretations are mostly on target, when we have demonstrated through empathic resonance that we have heard and understood what has been said, when we *prove* that we are trustworthy, competent, and ethical professionals as well as warm and authentic human beings, then we make a difference.

Warmth and genuineness are what moderate the perception of arrogance. For when we go too far, it is when our sense of self-assurance becomes so self-involved, so intrusive, that all perspective on reality is lost. The blending of confidence with humility creates a competent, confident human being, but one with doubts, confusions, and limitations that do not mar the overall image! The client feels as if he or she is in the presence of someone who is indeed quite special — someone who certainly has expertise and integrity, but more than that, someone who is so matter-of-fact about these attributes that they never need to be overtly mentioned. They are part of who the therapist is, and this confidence allows him or her to make the client feel special.

Patience

Clients do not come to us in a vacuum. They usually have a long history of being aided in life by well-meaning helpers. These may include the kindergarten teacher who "helped" them learn self-control by rapping their knuckles and scolding them in front of their peers. It may include their parents' efforts to teach them to swim by throwing them into the deep end of the pool. There have been thousands, perhaps millions of other "lessons" from their parents, relatives, friends, teachers, ministers or rabbis, neighbors, and a host of other sources, the least of which may have been other therapists. Clients have thus learned a great deal, but always with certain side effects that inhibit learning in the future. They come to us with these defenses, resistances, traumas, scars, and maladaptive patterns, as well as with whatever presenting complaint motivated the desire to seek help at this time.

Doing good therapy involves not only the willingness and capacity for acting decisively when the situation calls for it, but also the act of not acting when that is what is needed. People need time, at a pace all their own, to integrate new learnings, to build courage to experiment with new behaviors, to make sound decisions, and to work through their reluctance, apprehensions, and fears. We are asking them to give up something, an old ally, a friend who constantly gets them in trouble but a lifelong friend nevertheless, before they feel equipped to try something else that might work better. So we have to wait until they are utterly convinced there is nothing worse, that life is so awful the way it is that the only possibility for salvation is to try *anything* else other than what they are currently doing. And this can take a while.

Effective therapy moves at the pace of the client, not the clinician. Effective therapists are able to demonstrate a level of patience that supercedes their own needs to see observable movement and progress. They do this by tolerating the pauses and silences, allowing the client to assume responsibility for movement and content. They accept wherever the client is, not needing him or her to be different. And finally, they are not only patient with clients, but patient with themselves.

Of all the qualities that are part of being a compleat therapist, I struggle with patience the most. It is because I am not very tolerant of my own reticence that I have such a hard time waiting for clients to move at their own pace. Sometimes, it seems, I make the most brilliant interpretations that go unacknowledged. Sometimes, I *do* think I know what is best for a client—but try as I might to push, he or she will not budge until the time is right.

Rick was miserable working in his family business. He felt as though he would never be his own person as long as his father—a man who ruled harshly and unforgivingly—held him under his thumb. Rick could not respect himself under these circumstances, yet he could not bring himself to escape. "The problem seems simple enough," I ventured. "What will it take for you to be able to walk away and start your own life?"

When he informed me that what he primarily needed in therapy was a little push, I accommodated him. We spent the better part of several weeks making preparations for him to make his move, and because his course of action seemed so clear at the time, I neglected a more lengthy and time-consuming process of getting to know him and learning about where he came from and how he got to where he was. The man wanted support, and I was chomping at the bit to give it to him, especially since a few of my other cases were dragging on for years with no immediate end in sight. Here was an opportunity in which I could make a difference quickly, and that, after all, was why I became a therapist — to fix other people's problems, since as a child I felt so impotent with my own.

Rick *was* persuaded (or I suppose I convinced him) to leave his father's company and go off on his own to live happily ever after. Six months later he ended up back with his family business, more miserable and discouraged than ever. Then we began the more difficult task of trying to unravel some of the other issues that were at stake for him.

It was impatience that was the downfall for both of us. We wanted instant results — he, an immediate relief of pain, me, a quick cure to appease my own need to feel like a potent healer. Yet, only a few months earlier, I lost a client because I proceeded too cautiously. How could I ever find this balance?

Perhaps the outcome of all therapy comes down to this: either pushing too fast or too slowly. Clients give up when they either do not feel any structure, direction, and motivation from their therapist, or when they feel so much it goes beyond the threshold of what they can tolerate. So the trick is to be patient without being passive, to bring pressures to bear on the client, but only as much as can be handled at any moment.

This balance is very much like riding a bicycle, where we have to make innumerable minute adjustments every second to ensure that we stay upright and keep pedaling forward. When we feel the client drifting off, fading away, and feeling discouraged, we turn up the heat a bit with an interpretation or confrontation we believe he or she can handle. Now we have the client's attention again — his or her continued curiosity and commitment. Then we sense the client's fear; we can feel him or her bolting. And so we turn down the heat a notch. We offer encouragement and support. We stay with the client's feelings for a while. When the client lets us know he or she can handle a little more, the cycle begins anew, a little at a time.

Acceptance of Imperfections

In an analysis of fifty-eight personal accounts of critical incidents that shaped the development of counselors, Cormier (1988) found the most common theme to be the usefulness of mistakes and failures as an impetus for growth. This was also the central theme of a previous volume in this series on how therapists are able to accept their imperfections, to remain open to processing their mistakes and misjudgments, and to use them as a means of increasing their effectiveness in the future (Kottler and Blau, 1989).

Yalom (1989), for example, experienced a breakthrough with a seriously disturbed client by freely admitting to a miscalculation in comparing her to the homeless. Later, while he and the client were analyzing what had been the turning point in their work together, she confided that it was something very simple, seemingly inconsequential, but very significant to her:

> "What precisely," I asked, "was helpful to you in our last hour? At what moment did you begin to feel better? Let's track it down together."
> "Well, one thing was the way you handled the crack about the homeless. I could have used that to keep punishing you — in fact, I know I've done that with shrinks in the past. But when you stated in such a matter-of-fact way what your intentions were and that you had been clumsy, I found I couldn't throw a tantrum about it" [Yalom, 1989, p. 220].

So what helped Yalom to reach this particular client was his willingness to confront his own stupidity. As Welles (1988) has so convincingly demonstrated, history is replete with examples of supreme stupidity that have caused tremendous damage because of people's failure to admit mistakes and learn from them. He cites as a representative example the case of World War I generals who kept initiating frontal assaults because they believed that their strategy was perpetually sound; it was the execution of their plan that caused so many casualties.

This is, of course, the same reasoning that permits therapists to persist in applying their theories and interventions in the face of irrefutable evidence that client functioning is rapidly deteriorating. Ineffective therapists tell themselves: "There is nothing wrong with the approach I am following, nor with the way in which I am using it. Therefore, it must be the client's resistance/stubbornness/pathology/lack of motivation that is sabotaging progress. With sufficient time and patience, surely the client will come around."

In his review of the history of human stupidity, Welles concludes that failure is essentially a corruption of learning in which input becomes selective, feedback inaccurate, perceptions skewed, and cognitive schemata inflexible. When people are unable to recognize their errors, check results against expectations, and modify their behavior, unsuccessful outcomes occur.

Effective therapists remain successful much of the time because they are open to examining their errors instead of finding ways to disown them. Rather than blaming client resistance or making other excuses for things not going the way they were planned, they accept their limitations, the inevitability of things beyond their control, and they work hard not to repeat the same mistakes.

Consider, for example, the clinician who is so threatened by the possibility of failure that he or she practices defensively and never takes risks—preferring a safe, predictable, benign treatment that will not help all that much, but that will not hurt either. When the client does not improve, it is because of "resistance," "family interference," "poor motivation," "unconscious sabotage"—anything other than the therapist's own behavior or attitude. And because this stance does not allow for accepting the possibility of failures, such a therapist is destined to repeat them.

The best practitioners in any discipline are always those who

can identify their weaknesses, recognize when they are impeding progress, and find ways to work around them. This is true
of teachers, athletes, engineers, or philosophers. When Bertrand
Russell — ex-mathematician and philosopher extraordinaire —
turned to education as his next challenge, he discovered that
he was a dismal failure at running a school. His idealism, poor
business sense, self-absorption, and constant philandering made
him a poor educator and administrator. And yet this ill-fated
venture that plunged him hopelessly in debt became the impetus for him to develop as the consummate public communicator. Russell recognized he could not keep pace with the intellectual rigors of his Oxford contemporaries. His best works on logic
and mathematics had been published decades earlier. So he
turned his formidable talents as a writer and speaker to popu-
larizing philosophy for the masses, to introducing the average
person to the values of philosophical inquiry. By recognizing
what he could *not* do any more — that is, construct logical models
of human thought — Russell turned instead to what he *could* do
well: explain the works of other philosophers. His weakness,
once acknowledged, allowed him to concentrate his powers in
areas of his greatest strength.

In the most popular of all his works, a primer on the problems of philosophy, Russell, ([1912] 1959, p. 161) closed the
book with a summary that can be applied to the work of the
therapist as well: "Philosophy is to be studied, not for the sake
of any definite answers to its questions, since no definite answers can, as a rule, be known to be true, but rather for the
sake of the questions themselves; because these qualities enlarge
our conception of what is possible, enrich our intellectual imagination, and diminish the dogmatic assurance which closes the
mind against speculation; but above all because, through the
greatness of the universe which philosophy contemplates, the
mind also is rendered great, and becomes capable of that union with the universe which constitutes its highest good."

The therapist who discovers, like Russell, that there are certain areas of his or her craft that are troubling — perhaps a
difficulty with confrontation, or working through transference
conflicts, or taking too much responsibility for client growth —

can learn with honest self-scrutiny and supervision to improve these skills and work around any problems.

I am struck, for example, by how many times my work with clients becomes impeded by my intense need to be liked by everyone all of the time. I have worked on this issue in personal therapy and supervision on and off for decades. And I suppose I have made some progress: now when a student writes a poor course evaluation or a client "fires" me, it only sends me into a tailspin for days instead of weeks. I am certain I will continue to struggle with this issue all my life. But meanwhile, my work with clients occasionally suffers because my own need to have them like me gets in the way of doing some things that need to be done. For instance, I catch myself overreacting to any acting out on the part of an angry client. I tell myself on the inside that it is *only* a transference reaction, but I still take it personally. I act hurt. The client apologizes and backs off. And this fertile area of exploration becomes closed off. Now, knowing this about myself, but still unable much of the time to stop my own issues from getting in the way, I have learned to work around them. For one thing, I can now very reliably catch myself doing this and can thus take steps to deal with it in the session so that we can work on the client's transference issues or perhaps even genuine anger toward me. This is not where I would like to be with this issue; eventually I would like to work this through more fully. But in the meantime, I can work around it, and accept (or try to accept) this imperfection in myself.

There is a tremendous advantage to knowing the limitations of what we are able to do. There are some instances in which no matter what form and style of psychotherapy is practiced, the client is not going to significantly improve. Effective therapists are good at recognizing when they are being ineffective, when their efforts are not working. They are knowledgeable in general about those kinds of disorders that are very resistant to treatment by therapy alone. They are able to recognize these cases and the futility of proceeding with interventions that both the client and therapist realize are not much help. After several months of working with someone who has bipolar features or obsessive-compulsive behaviors or panic disorder that does not seem to be improving, the clinician will reach out to a medical colleague for consultation.

This willingness to ask for help is an important trait in compleat therapists. They are successful because they recognize what they do not know and cannot do, and because they have an intense desire to learn more through continued training, supervision, and peer consultation. If at some time every week (or every day in some cases), therapists do not feel stuck, at a loss as to how to proceed, confused and unsure about what is happening with clients, then they are probably neither very honest with themselves nor very open to confronting the limits of their capabilities.

The Key Importance of Sensitivity

One thing that therapists can do better than most people, and good therapists can do better than lousy ones, is observe nuances in human experience and communication. So much of what we do is to attend to the client's "felt sense" of what is going on inside. We listen intensely to the words that are spoken, interpreting surface and underlying meanings. We observe closely what clients do and say they do in the outside world, connecting these actions to our knowing of what they are like. In short, we do everything within our power to be what Rogers called empathic — the extraordinary sensitivity to whatever another person is experiencing at any moment. It is complete understanding without judgment.

The ideal therapist has, according to Bugental (1978), developed, trained, and polished sensitivity above all other attributes. Sensitivity is quite simply the use of all our senses (including intuition) to attend to whatever is happening: "That sensing is like a fine instrument, capable of picking up clues that the average person might not register: nuances of meaning, intonations of voice, subtle changes of facial expression or body posture, hesitations, slips of speech, and all the thousand and one subtle expressions of a person in the midst of life" (Bugental, 1978, p. 41).

One client, who has seen her fair share of therapists in her life, reviewed what the various practitioners did or did not do that she found especially helpful. For her — and most clients would heartily agree — effectiveness was based primarily on the therapist's capacity to be sensitive. In her words:

> I am remembering the therapists I have seen. First there was Dr. L. with this big desk and his aquarium and his couch that I refused to get near. He was lifeless and boring and our relationship was dry and sterile. I suspect one must be sensitive in order to be intuitive, and Dr. L. was far from sensitive. His favorite intervention was to harangue me for not having assumed my husband's name. He did understand the place of power in the therapeutic relationship, however, and its place was squarely in his hands. "See what I've done for you?" he was actually heard to say. I laughed in astonishment and walked out of his office.
>
> Years later, a fresh start with Dr. D. I see now that he understood something about being sensitive. He asked me to call him by his first name, and he let his own personality show through. He was warm and pleasant and gave me the sense that he really liked me. Looking back, I recognize that he used exquisite sensitivity in his work because he had an excellent sense of timing — he knew just when to say the right thing.
>
> And then there was Dr. S. Here was a therapist totally nourished by her sensitivity, totally alive in her powers of perception. I see now that about 90 percent of what she did for me, and with me, came from her skill at being incredibly sensitive. She created an atmosphere of expectancy in which I was caught up in knowing that breakthroughs were imminent. She somehow knew just how much I could handle at any moment in time. It was a pace of growth that I had always longed for. I soared. I stretched. I changed. And after a while, I noticed

that somehow, somewhere along the way, I too had learned to be extraordinarily sensitive.

All of the best qualities of the compleat therapist are contained in this last description. Sensitivity embodies all of the intangible dimensions of the therapist's personality—the power, the kindness and caring, and especially the ability to read accurately what is happening.

Effective therapists are excellent observers of behavior. They see, hear, and sense things that are not accessible to the untrained or unaware. They find patterns out of chaos, structures out of apparently unrelated events. They are witnesses who are able to see things as they are, who can recall significant details, and who can make sense out of a jamboree of confusing data.

A good therapist can see that the emperor is not wearing any clothes, and will not hesitate to tell him so: "I notice that it's hard for you to stop talking. Each time I attempt to respond to you, you do several things. First, you gesture with your hand. Second, you take breaths in the middle of your statements, as if you are afraid that if you paused at the end of a sentence, you might not be allowed to finish. It is as if you are communicating with your whole being that you are not used to being heard or allowed to speak freely and completely."

The sensitivity that allows a therapist to perceive subtle dimensions of a client's behavior is useless without the capacity to make sense out of what it means. The qualities of a therapist's personality are certainly important; but so are the distinctive ways in which we process information and the ways in which we make sense of the patterns we can recognize.

CHAPTER FIVE

How Therapists
Perceive, Think, Sense, and Process
Their Experiences

There was a time, long, long ago, when I was so anxious about doing psychotherapy, and so enamored of its complexity, that I was able to stay present with most of my clients practically all of the time. Sessions seemed over in a matter of a few brief moments. I was able to focus my concentration so totally on what clients were saying and doing that I, as a separate being, ceased to exist. I became so immersed in the activity of doing therapy, so intrigued by all its nuances, so fascinated by the experiences of my clients, that I could never have dreamed of leaving the room for more than a moment or two.

It is now many years later, and I notice quite a different phenomenon occurring: there is not a single client I see with whom I do not, at periodic intervals, tune out what they are saying and go off into my own mental world. Most of the time, these are fleeting moments — flash images that are provoked by something the client said or did. Yet with some clients who I find especially difficult to be with, I leave the room more often than I would like to admit. I am, of course, uncomfortable about these self-indulgent lapses that, while excusably human, are nonetheless unprofessional. I feel guilty that I am paid to listen to people, to give them my undivided attention, and sometimes I only pretend to fulfill my end of the contract. And I am curious about what this behavior, these trips inside my mind, say about

me. I wonder what other therapists do inside their heads when
they are not attending to the business at hand. Where do other
therapists go when they leave the room?

The whole subject of what goes on inside therapists' minds
is so interesting — not just when we are off into personal rever-
ies, but more so when we are really humming along with a client,
tracking speech patterns and nonverbal behavior, interpreting
underlying meanings, sorting out and making sense of what we
see, hear, feel and sense. And there is a distinctive way that
therapists who are most effective in their craft are able to use
their brains — a cognitive process that is both rational and intuitive, focused yet flexible. In short, professionals who are good
at helping people resolve their difficulties are able to think in
a multidimensional mode that transcends disciplinary boundaries. They stretch beyond conventional reasoning in ways that
allow them to discover patterns, apply their skills and knowledge, and perceive things that are invisible to all but the en-
lightened.

Multidimensional and Multidisciplinary Thinking

So much of what constitutes good therapy involves understanding and explaining complex, abstract phenomena in more
comprehensible terms. Most of our useful theoretical concepts
were derived from ideas borrowed from allied disciplines; these
ideas were then translated into instructive metaphors for our
own purposes.

Freud likened the psyche to the biological systems he was most
familiar with. He relied on the literature of Shakespeare, the
philosophy of Nietzsche, the science of neurology, and the in-
vestigative methods of anthropology to visualize the concept of
the unconscious as a place to excavate layers of awareness.

So many other concepts — such as homeostasis, systems theory, even the now common idea of "feedback" — are the result
of a cross-fertilization between the sciences, the arts, and our
own discipline. Theoreticians and therapist trainers such as Rollo
May (1986, p. 215) have proposed for many years that clinicians could best be trained by majoring in the humanities rather

than in psychology as undergraduates, since "it is the humanities which give them the myths and symbols with which each age sees and interprets itself." The study of history, literature, the arts, and philosophy prepare the student for understanding the past and future.

The best clinicians are thus intimately familiar with fields other than our own. They are fluent not only in the languages of psychopathology and developmental psychology, but of biochemistry, and other social sciences, and the humanities. Within the discipline of philosophy alone, therapists must be familiar with each specialty. We delve into the realm of metaphysics by attempting to formulate notions of universal reality, of how the world works. We are students of ontology in that we hope to discover for ourselves, and to facilitate in others, the basic structure and meaning of existence. Ethics, of course, plays an important role not only in guiding professional conduct, but in helping the client answer the questions, "What is right for me?" and "What ought I to do?" Logic is the basis for the scientific method and sound reasoning that are so much a part of clinical diagnosis and decision making. Finally, epistemology is that branch of philosophy concerned with the nature of knowledge. The pursuit of knowledge is of course central to almost every aspect of our enterprise.

Therapists think in multiple dimensions, constantly shifting from the concrete to the abstract and back again. One minute we are using a mathematically sound system of logic to reason through possible cause-effect relationship, and the next we are spinning a complex metaphorical tale to symbolize instructive concepts. From there we may drift to the principles of developmental stage theories, and then to a discussion of themes in a particular move or book. Finally, we move back into the realm of the sciences when we explore physical symptoms or medications.

Consider, for example, the case of a client manifesting symptoms of anxiety. Initially, we might conceptualize the problem in functional terms: How is the problem helpful to the client? What is the discomfort drawing attention to that the client has been avoiding? What are the symptoms communicating? What do they represent or symbolize?

We next move from the functional in our thinking to the pragmatic. We start collecting specific information that might be useful. "When do you feel most anxious?" "What is it like for you?" "When did the symptoms first begin?" "How do you and others react?" "What have you tried so far to cope with the problem?"

From this point the therapist can shift in a dozen different directions, depending on particular specialties and interests. Perhaps a discussion will ensue based on the therapist's devotion to cognitive/linguistic considerations: "What do you tell yourself about the problem?" "How do you talk to yourself when you first become aware that you are feeling anxious?"

An interest in history can play a part: "Who in your family has had a similar problem?" "Have you ever had a similar feeling before?" Perhaps there would be attention to biological factors: "What happens in your body when you feel anxious?" "What effects have various medications had on your symptoms?" Literature might be brought into the session, or at least metaphors, stories, and images that have been drawn from films, the theater, or books, to highlight a certain point: "Perhaps you recall from your college days in the sciences that the body reacts in protective ways even when it misinterprets the perception of danger. The sympathetic nervous system is at work creating the sweating, rapid heartbeat, and adrenaline rush that scare you so much; it does so because it is overreacting to cues that it thinks are life-threatening and is therefore preparing you to run or fight.

The therapist has now shifted back and forth between disciplines and dimensions, constantly drawing on all of the wisdom at his or her disposal. Just how broad that base of knowledge is will determine the degree of creativity that is possible and the number of choices that are available in the selection of an intervention or course of action.

Searching for Patterns

The multidimensional and multidisciplinary perspective that is part of the effective therapist's style of thinking allows him or her to take in a vast assortment of information and process it in such a way that it can be organized, interpreted, and acted on. There is a scientific training component to the education of most therapists because of the belief that it teaches us to think more logically while reducing biases (Arkes, 1981; Turk and Salovey, 1986). This, in turn, is supposed to facilitate objectivity in clinical reasoning and to control excessive subjectivity that is often seen as an impediment to successful outcomes.

Most training programs favor models that teach clinicians to function like behavioral engineers—learning to be familiar with structures, materials, and interaction effects. However, unlike the scientist who is concerned with verified truth and the discovery of new phenomena, the thinking processes of the effective clinician lean more toward the utility of gathering information: "A scientist uses the results of experiments as a stepping-stone to refine the underlying theory and to formulate new questions. A clinician usually sees her task as completed when a therapeutic option has been effective" (Kanfer and Schefft, 1988, p. 13).

Therapists seek to apply scientific principles, combined with intuitive flashes, in the discovery of forms and patterns that emerge as part of the therapeutic process. We do this by drawing connections between things that were said or done earlier on the one hand and current events on the other, identifying thematic elements in the content of sessions and tracking the sequence of events. So much of the cognitive activity inside a clinician's mind consists of a series of judgments (Brehm and Smith, 1986; Gambrill, 1990). Should I do this or that? Is this person psychotic or suicidal? What would be most helpful right now? How am I doing so far?

Clients present themselves and their stories to us in a way that has some meaning, however disguised it might be. As we listen carefully, and watch the process unfold, we are constantly trying to do two things simultaneously: stay with the client in the present moment without judgment, and make continuous evaluative decisions in our minds with regard to organizing and making sense of what we have heard.

Piaget offered us the concepts of assimilation and accommodation to describe cognitive functioning during information processing. That which cannot be assimilated into existing schematic structures must be accommodated by the creation of new categories of understanding. Someone who could overhear the inner workings of a therapist's mind would hear a lot of questions like the following: What is this similar to that I have seen before? How does this fit, based on what I already know about human beings in general and this person in particular? What is the big picture of which this is only a small part?

This distinctive style of process patterning is illustrated in the following case. A woman returns to treatment after a year's absence; earlier she worked on issues of marital adjustment for six sessions. *(What is she doing back again?)* She reports that she would like help with a particular problem that is disturbing to her. *(Why now?)* Although she has no difficulty driving her car anywhere in the city, there is one particular stretch of highway that causes her tremendous anxiety and discomfort. *(I wonder what that means?)*

As we get into things further, she brings up other issues — her job dissatisfaction and lack of direction in her life. *(What is the connection of these issues to her presenting complaint? What is the meaning of that special section of road?)* I ask her to describe that part of the highway: "It has very high walls, almost as if I am driving through a tunnel. There's no exit for several miles in any direction. It's also located real near where my parents live." *(Aha!)*

The client reports her family history as unremarkable: "Growing up was just like *Leave It to Beaver.* Both my parents are great. We've always had a good relationship." *(What is she not telling me?)*

We move along, and as our relationship progresses, she casually mentions that she can now drive on that stretch of road with minimal difficulty. However, now she reports she has trouble sitting in restaurants. *(There* is *a pattern here. But what is the connection?)* We explore issues related to her poor self-esteem and what it means to her to feel closed in by walls or trapped in a place she cannot escape from. She realizes the extent to which she seeks the approval of others for every decision she makes. *(What does she do to seek* my *approval?)*

Her latest issue is related to fears about a lump her doctor found in her breast. It is apparently benign, but the doctor wants to do a biopsy anyway. Should she get a second opinion? She seems unduly concerned about what is appropriate. She consults the opinions of everyone in her world and carefully relates each one of their reactions. (*Wait a minute! Something is missing. She has asked everyone what they think — everyone but her mother.*)

I ask her.

Anger. Tremendous rage.

And, finally, out with it: her mother has never trusted her judgment. As a child, her mother protected her utterly and completely. She learned not to trust herself or her own opinions. Everything was done for her, and anything she tried to do herself was undermined. As an adult, she feels incapable of taking care of herself or making her own decisions — the source of her symptoms and poor self-esteem.

I present this case precisely because it is so familiar to most of us. It illustrates the process of how we think during the therapy process: listening, sorting, framing, adding, deleting, organizing, compiling, trying out different approaches. There were many hints during the therapy process that could have highlighted the patterns of this woman's issues. And it only takes a few key pieces for the puzzle to reveal itself.

Would a dozen other therapists working with this client have reached the same place? It is doubtful, because there are so many possible explanations that could account for her problems and so many different ways to think about them. Nevertheless, all therapists think in terms of themes, patterns, and structures, even if we do not agree on what they should be called. If we are skilled at teaching the client about the therapy process, we do not even have to be the ones to discover the underlying structures; the client is fully capable of doing so herself or himself.

We attempt to teach clients to think in a special way, to look for recurrent themes, common denominators, significant factors, essences, and patterns. We ask clients to pay attention to the process that is unfolding in our relationship, to their feelings toward us, to their style of communication, to the way they interact with us. It is the mutual understanding of these structures, sequences, and patterns that forms the basis for much of the therapy (Rothenberg, 1988).

Rice and Greenberg (1984) describe the principles that underlie the therapist's discovery of process patterns. The object is to recognize recurrent phenomena—those episodes, that while not identical, occur with regularity in most therapy work. These include transference reactions, resistance, and moments of insight. The particular incidents that are studied in depth and the phenomena that are explored most fully are chosen on the basis of one's operating theory of change.

Clinicians give different weight to the importance of some client behaviors over others. There is a template overlay in the minds of most therapists, guiding us as to what to look for, what is significant, and what usually unfolds. While this operating theory can be helpful in signaling us what to watch for, it can also be a hindrance.

Spence (1982), a dedicated psychoanalyst, finds his or any general theory to be confining in that established rules of practice limit our ability to see things as they really are. This is because we are so busy trying to find patterns that we expect to see: "To the extent that the analyst is guided by certain kinds of presuppositions, he will tend to understand the material in a more restricted fashion. He is handicapped in his task of constructive listening by the search for certain kinds of universals, and if some of these universals never appear, or appear in somewhat different forms, he is handicapped even further. He may, for example, miss the interpretive opportunities of the moment while waiting for some vague shape of the future" (Spence, 1982, p. 293).

How does one operate in unknown territory without any sort of map? How does the therapist work in the mysterious, ambiguous, confusing maze of human suffering without some idea of general guidelines regarding origins, causes, and antidotes for the problems?

In answer to this dilemma, Spence (1982) feels it is crucial for a therapist to be a "pattern finder," not a "pattern maker" who is inclined to create reality from a biased interpretation of the facts. He explains that because the "truth" that clients describe as their experience is not really what occurred, and because the truth the therapist hears is not really what the client said, more and more degrees of distortion occur between narrative and historical truth. Those therapists who are able to use their theories as rough outlines rather than exact blueprints for what will emerge are able to exercise the degree of flexibility and openness that is needed to become a more accurate observer of reality.

Applying the Principles of Clinical Inference

What keeps us honest and accurate in our perceptions is the application of scientific principles to case analysis. This is the methodology that begins with the systematic study of all the background relevant to the presenting complaint, including what is known and has been tried before. Dependent variables that will be used to measure results are functionally defined. Predictions are made as to likely outcomes that may result from certain interventions. These hypotheses are tested by manipulating independent variables. Finally, results are evaluated and inferences are drawn as to what has been learned.

All in all, this is what therapists are introduced to in graduate school as The Scientific Method. It is presumed that such training teaches practitioners/scientists how to reason logically and how to frame questions that can be addressed empirically. While such a model is quite helpful in writing theses, dissertations, and articles, there are certain limitations of the application in clinical practice. For one thing, we cannot ever isolate variables and manipulate them one at a time. Nor can we take the time to do a thorough review of literature and data related to the case. And further, it is so hard to remain objective, detached, and uninvolved with the "subject" when we have spent so many intimate hours together sharing ideas and feelings.

Effective therapists do, however, adapt the empirical method to their thinking on a regular basis. It is what allows us to sort out all the data flowing in, to formulate impressions of what we believe is happening, and then to double-check it and alter our diagnosis and treatment plan to better fit the specific needs of the client. We also apply principles of scientific reasoning in formulating and trying out new hypotheses, relying on logic to solve problems, and most of all, by investigating which methods have been found to be most helpful through systematic research rather than solely based on intuition or single authorities (Gambrill, 1990).

Therapists who follow the hypothetico-deductive inference method of diagnostic reasoning tend to think about their cases as puzzles to be solved. Not unlike the way an internist might approach a complaint of abdominal pain, the therapist would formulate an initial conception of what he or she believes is going on based on the limited data available. For example, the client reports feeling anxious and uneasy. He is not sleeping well and is feeling restless. He worries a lot. I then generate an initial problem formulation of "anxiety neurosis" and begin to test a set of hyptheses to confirm or reject this conception. Further exploration becomes focused not just on a complete picture of the client's world and functioning, but more specifically on the evidence of symptomatology related to this diagnosis.

Obviously, there are some problems with this kind of clinical reasoning since one's initial perceptions of what is going on can act as self-fulfilling prophecies that may cloud a more complex configuration of reality. For example, in the case described above, I learned that the onset of anxious feelings occurred right after a major life transition. The client recently moved to the area and just moved into a new house and began a new job. Because the data appear to fit the initial hypothesis, I may very well stop the exploration process, convinced that I have gotten to the bottom of things.

After six months of treatment this client made mild but erratic progress, eventually leaving therapy when he had convinced himself that he felt much better. And indeed he did understand himself better, even if those infuriating anxious feelings were still around. By this time, I was thoroughly convinced it would just take more time and patience, and so I neglected to look beyond the obvious. For example, when the client went on vacation for a week and felt considerably better, I concluded: "You see, you get away from the stress of your job and look how much better you feel."

Yet the client persisted in explaining that he liked his work and did not feel especially tense at his office. I called this "denial."

The client, at this juncture, decided to stop the sessions for a while, since he was not improving much more. I called this "resistance."

Six months later the client called to schedule an appointment. Smugly, I replied, "Oh, I see you're finally ready to deal with your unresolved issues."

The client showed up for the session calmer and more relaxed than he had ever appeared before. Before I could even begin, the client explained that he was not interested in resuming treatment but had made this appointment as a courtesy, in that he felt I might wish to know what had transpired. It seems that the furnace in his house started making strange noises, and so he called a repairperson who tested the equipment's functioning and reported that there had been a leak. There was a dangerous level of carbon monoxide circulating through the heating system since he had been in the house. The maintenance person then asked him if he had been feeling strange since he moved in — any symptoms of restlessness, dizziness, anxiety, unease?

My persistence in holding onto an initial diagnosis kept me from remaining open to other possibilities, and most of all, from trusting my client's intuition as to what might be going on. While this is a highly unusual case example, and one in which we could hardly expect any therapist to discover the physical cause of the symptoms, it nevertheless illustrates how the therapist's overconfidence, arrogance, and rigidity can get in the way of clearer thinking.

According to Elstein (1988), the therapist can, however, make good use of this clinical inference method of thinking described earlier, in spite of the dangers described. He believes that effective therapists have several things in common in their thinking.

1. They are able to draw on a base of knowledge and expertise that is compiled and organized in such a way that it can be easily retrieved.
2. They are highly flexible and adaptable in their thinking. They are able to apply a basic set of principles in unique ways to novel situations. They are quite willing to change

course whenever the data do not fit (rational analysis) or something does not feel right (intuitive processes).

3. They have a sequence of procedural rules that are not easily articulated but that nevertheless guide thinking processes throughout interactions. Their clinical judgment consists of a series of logical and highly functional steps that are based on integrating previously successful and unsuccessful outcomes. Schön (1983) describes this effortless reflection-in-action as what allows all effective practitioners to go beyond standard applications of technique with recognizable problems to the ability to handle cases they have never seen before. This highly intuitive form of applying existing concepts to novel situations is the correction for routine action.

4. They are able to apply generally recognized principles of practice more efficiently than those with less experience or talent. Their observations are not only more accurate, but they come to them more quickly.

With these qualities inherent in their style of reasoning and problem solving, effective therapists are able to draw a number of inferences based on the limited information available to them at the time. This is illustrated by the following representative situations in which a therapist might demonstrate sophisticated reasoning processes.

1. *A definable pattern from seemingly unrelated data.* "You have said previously that things were always easy for you growing up. You also mentioned how prone you are to erupting in temper tantrums. Further, I have noticed that with me, you become impatient when I don't immediately grasp what you mean. When you put all this together, it seems to point to a man who tries to impose the unrealistically high expectations you have for yourself onto others."

2. *A set of hypotheses regarding treatment strategies that are based on initial impressions.* "It is unlikely that medication would work in a situation such as yours since your depression seems to come from a specifically induced episode—the loss of your

job. I think that if you give us both a few weeks to help get you back on your feet, you will find your sleep and eating patterns leveling off. I also think that asking your family to join us might be helpful. Then we can all begin to examine some options you might have."

3. *Probabilities that certain things are likely based on factors in evidence.* "I take your suicidal fantasies *very* seriously, However, because you have children who would be helpless without you around, because you don't have a definite plan as to how you would kill yourself, I don't think hospitalization is indicated just yet. Let's keep a close watch to see if things change. And of course you can either call me or check yourself in if you feel that would be helpful."

4. *Predictions of what may occur based on past performance.* "Somehow, I sense that by agreeing so readily to my suggestion, you are not all that committed to following through with it. I have noticed that has been a pattern when you want to sabotage yourself."

5. *Generalizations about people in general from the study of a single case.* "Now that you mention how uninhibited you are when you are alone, acting out fantasies, and talking to yourself in funny voices, I suspect that most of us inhabit a secret world in private."

6. *Generalizations to an individual based on knowledge of people in general.* "I can well appreciate the ambivalent feelings you have toward your wife as you go through this divorce, especially with all of the mixed messages you have been getting from her. It isn't all that unusual that you would feel such adoration and rage toward her at the same time. It is not even so rare that the two of you would end up in bed again before this separation process is completed."

7. *A universe of possible meanings ascribed to a single behavior or situation.* "This silence has been continuing for some time and you seem at a loss as to how to break out of it. I have been wondering to myself whether you are taking time to process what has happened so far, whether you are deciding where you want to take things next, whether you are confused about what we just discussed, whether you are waiting for me

to rescue you, or whether you are testing me in some way to determine if I am worth trusting."

8.   *The features of a case or narrative that are most significant and relevant.* "You have presented a lot of information during the past hour—that you are experiencing marital problems, that your job is in jeopardy, and that recently you started to lose sleep and become depressed right after your boss put you on probation. We will have plenty of time to explore those issues later. For right now, I am especially interested in the history of bipolar disorders in your family. And you also mentioned that several years ago you had an episode very similar to this one, although at the time there was nothing you could point to that provoked it. I think before we proceed further with our therapy it would be a good idea for you to get a psychiatric consultation."

9.   *Things that may have occurred in the past based on present levels of functioning.* "When I just pointed out to you something you were doing, you jumped all over me as if I were attacking you. It seems like you have been brutally criticized by someone close to you before."

10. *Things that may occur in the future based on present levels of functioning.* "I know you are having a good day and are thus trying to convince yourself that the worst part is over. And I don't mean to discourage you, but I think it's a safe assumption that setbacks are inevitable. The new strategies you are practicing at home are still a bit awkward for you so it is going to take a while before you get the results you want."

Each of these inferences allows the therapist to diagnose accurately what clients are experiencing. They even allow us to infer when inferring is not appropriate and it is time to go with something else. The complicated process of diagnostic thinking, for example, involves much more than applying the principles of hypothetico-deductive reasoning.

Forming Diagnostic Impressions

To do good therapy, the clinician must be skilled at figureing out what is going on with a client, what the difficulty is, what is contributing to the problem, and what will probably be most helpful in alleviating it. This diagnostic impression is formed by some therapists within the first thirty to sixty seconds after meeting the client (Gauron and Dickinson, 1969), and most therapists create some kind of preliminary diagnosis within the first three minutes (Sandifer, Hordern, and Green, 1970).

We form such quick impressions as much to alleviate our own discomfort with ambiguity and uncertainty as for the client's good. Each client who walks in might be the one we cannot help. We may wonder whether we will know what to do. Will this be beyond our expertise? So there is immediate relief after settling on a working diagnosis. It is not usually the one we will stay with, but it helps us get a start with something familiar before we begin to explore the unknown.

This initial diagnostic formulation gives us a conceptual framework to begin systematic explorations and hypothesis testing. We start by noting, "This is a depression. There's no apparent severe personality disturbance. Appears to be functioning reasonably well. Has good relationships with others." We can then pin things down further: "Is the depression reactive or endogenous? Acute or chronic? Intermittent or continuous?"

It is not that there is anything especially wrong with forming an immediate impression of the client, but effective therapists will let this impression go in the face of new and contradictory data: "The client did use the word 'depression' to describe the way he had been feeling, and indeed some of his symptoms like loss of sleep and appetite seem to be vegetative signs. But he's been taking medication for high blood pressure. And he calls *everything* depressed that doesn't meet his expectations. In fact, his self-obsession and narcissism are what seem to be his primary problems."

Arnoult and Anderson (1988) describe the ways effective therapists are able to reduce biases in their thinking, such as faulty causal inferences or the persistence of erroneous beliefs. They are able to counteract their tendencies to form inaccurate decisions by generating multiple cause-effect relationships to keep thinking open and flexible (differential diagnosis). And they do not jump on the first idea and stay with it in the face of conflicting

data. They demonstrate a healthy degree of doubt and uncertainty: "What am I missing? What don't I know? What can't
I explain or account for?"

In a previous section we examined the process of pattern
search in the context of how a therapist characteristically thinks
and organizes the flow of data that stream in. The goal of this
mental activity is to discover meaningful aspects of the way the
client thinks, feels, or behaves as a clue to what the problem
is and what needs to be changed. As is true with so many other
applications in our field, there are tremendous variations in the
particular way this pattern search takes place.

Beitman (1987) reviews some of the clusters/variables/themes
that therapists tend to look for in their diagnostic observations.
Psychoanalysts spend their time in sessions thinking about what
defenses are operating in the client, what symbols are evident
in dreams, or what transference reactions are being acted out.
The cognitive therapist is searching for patterns of speech that
indicate underlying dysfunctional behavior. The existentialist
is processing patterns of core issues related to meaning, freedom, and responsibility. Even the educational consultant is assessing developmental patterns that have evolved over time.

There is, then, a matrix for observing the world that most
therapists subscribe to. The details of this model — that is, whether
attention is devoted to parent-adult-child transactions or linguistic patterns of communication — are relatively unimportant. But
the *process* of diagnostic thinking is remarkably universal. Effective therapists tend to do the following things, though not necessarily in the same order: (1) allow data, observations, perceptions, and experiences to flow into the brain; (2) organize the
information into temporary clusters that suggest hypotheses for
exploration; (3) make inquiries to facilitate study in particular
directions; (4) eliminate possibilities of what is *not* likely to be
occurring; (5) match what is observed with existing schematas
that have been experienced before; (6) make predictions as to
what is likely to occur, if a given pattern seems to be in evidence; (7) note inconsistencies and exceptions that make this
particular situation unique; and (8) apply the pattern formu-
lated to the guiding matrix.

Examples of this thinking process occur all the time in our drive to find meaning in behavior. A student schedules a conference to discuss one of her class papers. The matrix that suggests itself to me is one in which I expect a variation of: "This-grade-isn't-fair-you-messed-up-and-you'd-better-fix-it." I steel myself for the expected assault.

The student seems unusually contrite and timid. I alter the pattern a bit, but retain the matrix I favor in these situations: she is using guilt instead of aggression to get me to back down. All of this speculation, of course, has taken place before she has ever opened her mouth.

We begin. It is evident this meeting is not about her paper at all. Brilliant diagnostician that I am, I notice she does not even have *any* papers with her! In fact, she looks more like a client about to unload rather than a student. I notice she closed the door. She is twisting her hands in anguish.

It is time for a different matrix and a whole other set of possibilities; she wants me to listen and understand her. She wants a referral to a therapist. She wants advice. I notice it is my own anxiety about the unexpected situation that is leading me to rush ahead with solutions. I take a deep breath. And everything inside my head drifts into smoke. All this diagnostic stuff has interfered with my ability to simply observe and be with her. I suspend thinking for a while and just watch, listen, probe a little.

During the course of speaking aloud what she has memorized to say to me, the student drops her pencil. I bend to pick it up and reach over to hand it to her, feeling attentive and caring. She cowers in her seat and starts sobbing. I reach a little closer with the pencil and she screams. Unbidden, one thought immediately jumps into place: sexual abuse. I am not sure why I think this just yet. But now I have my matrix again. I start looking for the data to support this possibility and suggest ways I might be helpful.

This process of diagnostic thinking follows certain integrative constructs employed by most clinicians (Millon, 1988). Most therapists believe, for example, that: diagnoses are labels of convenience that approximate (but do not actually reflect) patterns of behavior; there are no rigid boundaries between diagnostic entities, no pure forms of psychopathology; symptoms are best understood in the context of specific situations and personalities; the clinical attributes that make up a particular diagnosis have structural (self-image, temperament, and other semipermanent properties) and functional components (cognitive style, psychodynamics, and other expressive modes).

Diagnostic thinking involves both the structural, self-image aspects of the client's personality and functional, interpersonal behavior. In the case of a histrionic, for instance, structural attributes would include being gregarious, charming, pleasure oriented, and busy, while functional attributes would include being flirtatious, manipulative, vain, dramatic, and demanding. The therapist is thus able to target treatment efforts toward the totality of the client's plight, including all dimensions of the problems — cognitive style, dysfunctional behaviors, interpersonal dynamics, self-image, characteristic moods, and psychodynamics. This merging of diverse elements into a unified method of information processing covers much more than the integration of structural and functional diagnostics. It also includes combining scientific, empirical methods — which rely on logic and objectivity — with heuristic and phenomenological approaches that access intuitive processes.

Thinking Heuristically

Rothenberg (1988, p. xii) sees the essence of effective therapy as a paradox in that the best clinicians are scientific, objective, rigorous, consistent, and logical, yet they are also highly imaginative: "They are scientific and rely on systematic data and theory, and they are aesthetic in their application of intensity, narrative, interpretation, and leaps of understanding."

Heuristic thinking is the core of subjective perception — the unique, personal, individual way of processing experience through private filters. When I am functioning heuristically I become aware of what is happening inside me in response to my client. I can feel tension or frustration or confusion, and by sharing my awareness, I can help the client to gain greater access to his or her own inner sensings.

Douglass and Moustakas (1985, p. 40) describe the heuristic method as "a search for discovery of meaning and essence in significant human experience." Derived from the Greek root *eureka* (as in the exclamation of insight and discovery), heuristics forms the basis for a subjective search for truth and understanding. It is similar to phenomenological thinking in that both view subjectivity as the basis for discovering truth, but different in that phenomenological truth seekers detach themselves from the investigation in order to perceive what is occurring more clearly, while heuristic practitioners immerse themselves completely in the journey. This is done to connect all aspects of experience through personal involvement and to enlarge the essence of an issue rather than seeking to reduce it. "Phenomenology ends with the essence of experience; heuristics retains the essence of the person in experience" (Douglass and Moustakas, 1985, p. 43).

The therapist (or researcher) employing this process helps the client conduct an exhaustive search of self through detailed descriptions of experience and provocative dialogue. While this method begins from a highly subjective, personal perspective, after data are generated, systematic and structured paths are taken to organize, explore, and make sense of what has been discovered. It is passion that is personally driven that distinguishes heuristics from other methods of inquiry.

The process is not complex, but quite natural and self-evident. Hunches and intuition are substituted for hypotheses, neutrality replaced by conviction: "Heuristics is concerned with meanings, not measurements; with essence, not appearance; with quality not quantity; with experience, not behavior" (Douglass and Moustakas, 1985, p. 42).

Anytime a therapist or scientist abandons the rigors of empirico-deductive reasoning for the greater freedom of personal problem solving, he or she is likely to follow a path that includes an immersion in the problem or issue, an internal dialogue about the nuances of the theme, and a verification of internal perceptions by synthesizing them with others' experience. It is a way of thinking that encompasses the total spectrum of experience — affective as well as cognitive processes, intuitive as well as analytic dimensions. It is spontaneous, free-flowing, moving in a rhythm, pace, and direction that, while self-directed, has a life and purpose of its own. When the clinician trusts this inner knowing and allows the internal wisdom — the tacit dimension of unconscious creativity — to lead and prod, he or she arrives at the truth in a most startling way.

The therapist who operates heuristically, either occasionally or routinely, begins with the recognition of an "itch." "Something is not quite right about this case. Something does not ring true. Something is out of balance. Things do not feel right. *I* do not feel right."

Immersion is the first step in which the therapist begins to explore the problem through an internal self-search that includes a gradually deepening and intensification of layers of awareness. "I feel uneasy about the way things are going. Yet the client appears satisfied. What in me feels unsettled? It's like I feel phoney, as if I'm pretending something. A flash of images raced by — of me playing a role in my sixth-grade play. I had a dance part and I was supposed to do a number with my partner, who was a girl I especially liked. I accidently ripped my pants just before it was our turn to go on. I felt so embarrassed I tried to back out. But the teacher/director told me nobody would notice. That I should pretend everything was fine, and the audience would believe it as well.

"So why does that come back to me now? What in me has been touched by this client who appears so serene, and yet is seething inside? What am I missing that is right in front of me yet beyond what I can see?"

Polanyi (1967) called this gaining of access to hidden meaning a process of *indwelling,* in which we allow certain images, feelings, and ideas to incubate within us. By immersing ourselves totally and completely in the issue, we are able to dwell on those dimensions that catch our attention and tug at our consciousness.

At no single clear point, the therapist moving through heuristic inquiry will eventually gravitate toward a general or specific direction. Understanding of the phenomena is elaborated by reaching out beyond the self to collect more data. Relying on the "tacit dimension" described by Polanyi (1967), the therapist senses that a particular line of exploration with the client may prove useful, without quite knowing why or how; to analyze the process would be to stop the flow of it. This *illumination* phase sparks an inner voice that is quietly urging: "I have been feeling uneasy about something as you were speaking, and I'm not exactly sure why. I just got this image, a feeling that what we're doing right now isn't quite consistent with what's going on inside of you. I can't exactly explain what you are doing or saying that doesn't appear congruent or authentic, but I just sense that part of you is pretending something you aren't really experiencing. What are you feeling right now as I'm saying this, and what images come to mind for you?"

The essence of tacit knowledge is to trust one's intuition without questioning or judging it. Yet once aware of a problem, the therapist must check it against the client's experience through self-disclosure, openness, dialogue, and, most of all, interaction.

A *synthesis* phase comes next. Information and understandings that have been processed internally and with the client must somehow be integrated. The new data are not classified, organized, or analyzed as in empirical deduction or even phenomenological reduction; instead, the essence of the experience is preserved. The therapist seeks to integrate the new learning for himself or herself, as well as facilitating a parallel process for the client. The thinking moves from fragments to a unified whole, from the specific to the general, from the individual to the universal, from appearances to essences, from raw data to meaningful themes, from a previous conception to a new reality: "What we both have experienced and now understand is that sometimes it is better to feel the raw pain, the shame and fear, and to work through the feelings to a place of self-acceptance than to deny the discomfort and pretend a self-assurance we don't feel."

The compleat therapist is able to think as an intuitive scientist who can reason both inductively and deductively, systematically uncovering mysteries, yet who has developed the tacit dimension, who trusts and uses inner forms of knowing. The clinician, thinking either heuristically or phenomenologically, is able to suspend all judgments in order to enter the client's world with perfect clarity.

This process of "epoché" was developed by the phenomeno-logical philosopher Edmund Husserl as a way "of returning to the self to discover the nature and meaning of things as they appear, and in their essence" (Moustakas, 1988, p. 2). In order to get at this purest form of knowledge, all supposition, precon-ceptions, theories, and other ideas that might interfere with pure listening must be suspended. The epoché process is one in which the therapist temporarily stops all thinking whatsoever, all in-tellectual problem solving, hypothesis testing, reasoning and analyzing, in order to open himself or herself up to the pure immediacy and spontaneity of relating to another person. It is a meditative state, a form of effortless concentration that allows us to see and hear and feel what is occurring within the client from a fresh and receptive perspective: "to focus on just what manifests itself in consciousness, to let things appear as such, let them linger and reveal themselves in their own time, nature, and meaning" (Moustakas, 1988, p. 111).

Thinking Metaphorically

The value of metaphorical thinking is self-evident to mem-bers of our profession. We must continually make shifts from one perspective to another, transcribing properties from one plane to another. We use metaphors to clarify, to describe com-plex ideas, to stimulate interest, to connect images with feel-ings, and to integrate the abstract with the concrete (Rothen-berg, 1988). In a symposium on the uses of metaphor in therapy DiGiuseppe (1988) explains: "A metaphor is like a solar eclipse in that it hides an object, but reveals its most salient character-istics when viewed through the right telescope. It enlightens while it obscures in order to appreciate better the subtle characteris-tics of a subject."

Napier (1988), for example, describes the case of a couple who began arguing in the car on the way to a scheduled mari-tal session. When they first entered the car, the wife discovered a piece of tar on the floor that she began to examine carefully. The husband disgustedly ordered her to throw it out the window. She steadfastly refused. An argument quickly escalated until they were both steaming by the time they entered Napier's office. Their starting point became an exploration of the significance of their heated interchange over a "black spot" that the wife had become attached to and did not want to relinquish.

Napier (1988, p. 4) says further: "This couple did not have a conscious plan to deal with this problem. The conflict emerged symbolically, and the 'dark spot' was unconsciously chosen to represent their difficulty with this issue. It was a mutually defined metaphor, or symbol, for the conflict, and it was not until we all deciphered the meaning of the metaphor that we could get to work on the emerging difficulty in their marriage."

The average clinical practice is replete with other illustrations of how metaphors can not only be used to represent patterns of dysfunctional behavior, but also as dramatic forms of communication. Graham and I had been going around and around for some time, like dogs circling one another for an advantage, but neither one making any headway. This was the same client who I introduced in the Preface, the man who challenged me to explain how and why therapy works. For months we had been locked in a struggle that I did not know how we had gotten into, much less had any inkling of how to extricate myself from.

The conflict, in all its various manifestations, went something like this: Graham would demand that I provide more structure to our sessions, more guidance for the direction he should take in his life. I would explain, patiently and methodically, that my role was as a consultant, and that ultimately *he* would have to make his own decisions. The fact that he could not tolerate the ambiguity and freedom inherent in our encounter was a clue as to why he could not take charge of his life outside of therapy.

Forever concrete and regimented in his thinking, he would cry out in exasperation: "How can you just sit there watching me suffer and not *do* anything to help? You are the expert. You went to school for many years and have been doing this work for a long time. I know you could give me advice, or at least, more direct answers to my questions — but you continue to play those games of being so withholding. Why do I come to you if you won't help me?"

I would then tell Graham all over again about how even if

I did know what was best for him, and I agreed to tell him what to do, I would only be reinforcing the idea that he does not know what is best for himself, that he needs someone else to tell him what to do with his life. I further explained that he would only become more dependent on me the next time he was confused. While all of this sounded quite eloquent and convincing to me, he just refused to hear it. And so we went round and round.

The inspiration for our breakthrough literally came out of left field. For while I was talking I had been staring over his shoulder out the window of my office — which happens to overlook a Little League baseball field. The baseball metaphor began to take shape in my mind, since it brought together so many elements we had been discussing. The last piece of the puzzle was to personalize the metaphor in such a way that he could not block out the message. And since the whole focus of Graham's life was his nine-year-old son, even that last piece fell into place.

"Graham, you keep asking me why I don't help you. And I have explained over and over that I *am* helping you just the way a coach is supposed to help — by teaching fundamentals. In your case, these basics consist of your learning to live with uncertainty and to make your own decisions.

"You see that baseball diamond out the window? Imagine that your son approached you and asked you to teach him to hit to the opposite field — in his case right field. There you are, out there on the field, pitching to him. Each time he hits the balls to left field, you refuse to retrieve them. Instead, you make him put the bat down and stroll all the way out there to get the balls *even though you are closer.* He complains each time: 'Dad, why can't *you* do it? It would save us time, and some of the balls are just a few feet away from you. This doesn't make sense.'

"But it does make perfect sense to you as his coach. For each time he walks out to left field to retrieve the balls that went awry, he has to think about what he did wrong and concentrate on what he has to do next time. Although it takes longer in the short run to complete your exercises, he will eventually learn to correct himself in order to avoid the consequences of paying for his mistakes."

The smile on Graham's face told me immediately that he *did* understand. "So what you're saying as my coach is that the reason you don't offer easy answers is so that I will learn, even though it's frustrating and time consuming, to find my own answers?"

Yes, that's exactly what I had been telling him over and over for a long time. But until then, I couldn't get through. Whether it was really the power of the metaphor that made the difference, or some other variable that altered his readiness to face this issue of self-responsibility, I will never know. But images such as this one are often associated with breakthroughs because they enable clients to recall vividly constructed examples that can be accessed on demand.

As clients describe their experiences, we are constantly making shifts inside our minds, asking ourselves: "What is this like?" "What is another way to describe the same thing?" "What's an example of the point I would like to make?" "How can I translate this concept to one that will connect with the client's experience?" Or, for those who operate less analytically, intuitive urgings will do their part to push to the forefront of awareness an instructive metaphor that fits with what is being discussed.

A client with panic disorder becomes immobilized by the first stirrings of any associated symptoms. As soon as she notices (and of course she is hypervigilant) the slightest sensation reminiscent of speeded-up heart rate or constricted breathing, she brings on herself a full-fledged "attack" by terrifying herself with thoughts that she is completely out of control. Her fear is further intensified by her frustration in making any kind of sense out of the symptoms. She refused any type of medication whenever it was offered, taking the more courageous stand of finding out what her body was trying to communicate to her. However, until such insights could be reached, she was teetering on the edge of stable functioning, fearful at any moment she could be immobilized. She desperately searched for an explanation for what she was experiencing. It is, therefore, the therapist's task to help her think metaphorically about her symptoms in such a way that they will not be experienced as so disturbing to her. The following explanation is an example of an attempt to conceptualize the symptoms in a manner that is not so alarming.

"A long time ago whenever human beings faced danger, such as the prospect of being eaten by a saber-toothed tiger, the body equipped itself with a means for escape or defense. When the brain perceives imminent danger, the sympathetic nervous system kicks in gear to offer you better protection. The heart rate speeds up to pump more oxygen through the muscles you will be using to run or fight. Your breathing rate increases as well. The eyes dilate to improve vision. The digestive system closes down to divert energy to more useful places. Your mouth becomes dry, your stomach fluttery. Adrenalin pumps through your body providing extra bursts of power, but with the side effects of quivering limbs. Your body is responding to orders from your brain, which is overreacting to perceived stress. It is doing everything in its power to mobilize your resources to do battle.

"So whenever you start to feel these symptoms, remind yourself there really is not a saber-toothed tiger that is threatening you, and that your body is simply misinterpreting signals from your mind, orders that *you* can change."

So much of our internal energy during sessions is taken up with either attending to what the client is communicating or converting the descriptions that are presented to metaphors that we can do something with. Some of those that are most appropriate, we pass on to the client in the form of reframing their concerns or packaging them in ways that are helpful; many others we keep to ourselves. We have a private dialogue going on inside our heads, one that communicates in the language of metaphors, symbols, representations or what we see, feel, and sense. All of this takes place in order that we may tidy up all the information at our disposal, and thus concentrate on helping the client discover what it means.

Operating Intuitively

All of the intangible components of what makes an effective therapist — the hunches and feelings and senses about what is happening — can be lumped together as intuition. Whereas rational thought is that part of us that diagnoses, analyzes, examines, investigates, and dissects, intuitive thought observes, listens, feels, takes in without evaluation, and then simply *reacts*.

About intuition Anne Morrow Lindbergh (1955, p. 17) said: "One never knows what chance treasures these easy, unconscious rollers may toss up, on the smooth white sand of the conscious mind. . . . But it must not be sought for or — heaven forbid! — dug for. No, no dredging of the seabottom here. That would defeat one's purpose. The sea does not reward those who are too anxious, too greedy, or too impatient. To dig for treasures shows not only impatience and greed, but lack of faith. Patience, patience, patience is what the sea teaches. Patience and faith. One should lie empty, open, choiceless as a beach — waiting for a gift from the sea."

These intuitive gifts, however, are only available for those who have sufficiently mastered their fields. It is only the expert who can take a dozen separate steps of the beginner, and in a single leap, find the essence of a problem. Benderly (1989, p. 36) for example, describes the process of intuition in the case of a physician's thinking processes: "An experienced doctor takes one look at a spotty, feverish child and instantly diagnoses measles. A young intern looks at the same patient but takes far longer to arrive at the same diagnosis, methodologically eliminating chicken pox, German measles, and scarlet fever. The experienced doctor's analysis is fast and accurate; she constructs the investigation around a comprehensive view of possibilities, unlike her junior colleague who must move through a series of small ad hoc decisions."

Intuition, then, is a form of organized experience that allows effective therapists to access knowledge and find meaningful patterns. It is relied on, not as a substitute for rational thought processes, but as the springboard that initiates them, or as the guide that validates whether we are headed in the right direction. Goldberg (1983, p. 34) could have been talking directly to therapists in his book on intuition when he said: "When we attempt to be logical in complex situations, when we are forced to deal with incomplete information, unfamiliar subject matter, or ambiguous premises, we are dependent on intuition to tell us whether we are on the right track."

Common to those with heightened sensitivity, intuition represents all the predictions and interventions we make without being able to explain fully just how we know. That is not to say
that we do not make something up that sounds reasonable if
we are challenged to account for our behavior. But when we
are *really* honest with ourselves, we *know* that it was not just a
"lucky guess," nor was it a deliberately and carefully thought-
out plan. In fact, we do not really know what it was. One minute
we were just buzzing along in a session, doing what we usually
do, and then, before we quite knew what was happening, some
strange idea just popped into our head. One therapist relates
this example of an intuitive experience:

> I was sitting with my office partner at the end of
> a typically full, volatile day. We were reviewing our
> cases with one another when, out of the blue and
> seemingly apropos of nothing, I said to her as she
> was describing one of her clients: "You need to
> check the boy out carefully. Watch him for any
> marks or bruises. I sense that he may somehow be
> hurt." She asked if I was concerned with abuse, and
> I replied that I was more worried that he would
> harm himself. I have no idea why I said that or what
> I was basing these feelings on. I had never met the
> boy before, and I had only heard the briefest of
> descriptions of his issues. Nothing my partner re-
> lated to me indicated the slightest impression he was
> at risk, and when she pressed me for an explana-
> tion, I could give her none.
>
> The next morning as I walked into the office I
> was met by my partner, who appeared quite shaken.
> She informed me that the boy I was concerned
> about had showed up for his session with his wrist
> bandaged. He reported that he had "accidentally"
> fallen on a broken piece of glass (in an unlikely way)
> and nearly severed the artery.

So what was this all about? Coincidence? Had this therapist
picked up the apprehensions in her partner that she was una-

ware of as she described the case? Was this "intuition" a case of preconscious hypersensitivity to certain cues?

While hardly in as dramatic a way, most therapists put their intuitions and hunches to work on a daily basis. "When you arrive at a conclusion through rational thought you can usually trace the mental process backward and identify the antecedent steps. Intuition is inexplicable" (Goldberg, 1983, p. 33). Or at least the process is so complex, elusive, and abstract that our present levels of sophistication and knowledge make analysis difficult — and perhaps even undesirable since once we begin to analyze or explain intuition we begin to lose its power.

Hayward (1984) speaks of the imbalance in the thinking of most scientists and professionals when they strongly favor logic over intuition. This leads to fragmentation, quantification, abstraction — separateness from the essence of what is experienced.

Intuition, if taken too far, also creates its own problems — mostly a lack of clarity and precision. But it also adds another dimension of power to our thinking. Intuition involves an interconnection among all the nonconceptual elements that are beyond our awareness and consciousness. It thus gives us access to not only things we already know, but to a whole universe of possibilities that are currently beyond our grasp.

Reason and intuition are complementary in the effective therapist's mind. They feed off one another. They validate the truth of what the other infers. One encourages and supports the expansiveness of the narrow belief of the other. And when applied together, they provide the high degree of flexibility that is so important to therapeutic work.

Functioning Flexibly

While over a half century of empirical research has not been able to demonstrate the superiority of one therapeutic approach over another, it has been very clearly determined that certain kinds of interventions and clinical styles are likely to be more effective with particular clients. Change is multidimensional (Lambert, Shapiro, and Bergin, 1986).

It has been fairly well documented in the literature that certain phobic reactions are especially responsive to behavior therapy, that sexual dysfunctions are best treated with a combination of sensate focus exercises and insight therapy, that bipolar symptoms and endogenous depressions are most amenable to psychopharmacological treatment, that relationship-oriented insight therapy is best for those with unresolved internal struggles. Even on a more pragmatic level, most clinicians notice that some clients tend to do better than others with particular kinds of interventions. Even if we remain "true to our school," there are still many possible treatment methods.

Craig (1986), who identifies himself quite strongly as an existential therapist, was nevertheless taken aback when asked to cite the single key variable in his work with clients. For although he embraces a set of assumptions about what constitutes good therapy, he does not apply them in the same way more than once. Some clients seem to need more overt support than others. Some respond better to more or less active involvement on the part of the therapist, or more or less structure.

Garfield (1980, p. 187) feels that flexibility is the cornerstone of a therapist's effectiveness: "This should not be interpreted to mean that the therapist simply flies by the seat of his free associations or intuitions. The therapist should have some hypotheses to guide him and some tentative plan for therapy. However, as already emphasized, he has to be ready to test his hypotheses as time goes on and be willing to modify them in the light of new observations and information." Although Garfield sees some problem with a process as "unscientific" as intuition, it is very often a hunch, a feeling, or an image that leads us to give up a particular course of action and try something else.

In short, the therapist's flexibility allows for the ideal match between what a particular client needs at a given moment of time — whether it is confrontation or reassurance, structure or permissiveness — and what the clinician is able to deliver. Alexander and French (1946) concluded long ago that the single most important variable in helping treatment to proceed in an efficient and effective manner is the clinician's own flexibility.

Among other things, this flexibility requires an egalitarian outlook. Therapists need to be flexible in the sense of being accepting, open, and nonjudgmental. Flexibility also operates in therapists' choice of interventions.

Behavior therapists would define this in terms of specific techniques that are at their disposal. They would thus attempt to familiarize themselves with as many intervention strategies as possible, employing one method with migraine headaches, another with enuresis, still another with school phobia or insomnia. On the other hand, insight-oriented practitioners—who eschew technique-oriented styles—practice their craft with a high degree of adaptability to a given issue, client, or circumstance. This flexibility promotes greater effectiveness because of the therapist's ability to change just as the client changes. Any marriage will conclude unsatisfactorily when only one partner changes and the other remains the same. So while the therapist does show a certain stability or even predictability in his or her behavior, there is also much room for maneuvering. This allows the therapist to be active or passive, lighthearted or sober, witty or sincere, loving or stern, or warm or disconnected, depending on just what is called for. The essence of therapeutic effectiveness is to know or sense what might work and to be flexible enough to change directions in mid-course to more effectively address what is going on.

If we could enter the mind of any therapist while conducting a session, it is likely we would witness an inner dialogue that goes something like this:

Okay. Where were we? Oh, yeah. She was talking about . . . Oh oh. Her face is clouding up. Something is going on. Wonder what it is . . .

"I notice that your face changed as you were talking, as if you were saying one thing but thinking quite another."

Not bad. Short. Sweet. Accurate. But she's not buying it. Why is she shaking her head? Could I have misread her? I doubt it.

"You shake your head, yet you don't look very convincing . . . ?

Oops. I'm not listening to her. Even if she is denying something, that is her right. I'm pushing her too hard. Time to back off.

"When I interrupted you earlier, you were talking about . . . "

Just stay with her. She's not ready yet to face what she is avoiding. But she looks bored. As if she's reading her lines, taking up time to get through the session. But if I confront her with that, she'll just deny it. I'll wait awhile and see what happens.

"So you are feeling like . . . "

Enough is enough! This isn't working. Even if she's okay with this, I can't go on any longer with this game. I need to tell her that.

"Excuse me. Much of the time you have been talking, I have been aware of what has been going on inside of me. It feels very much like we are both . . . "

Ah, I see. I got her attention. She looks intrigued by what I said. But she essentially ignored the message I presented and focused instead on the part she is comfortable with. Maybe I should . . .

What is clear in this inner dialogue is the therapist's willingness to monitor what is happening for the client as well as personally. In doing this, the therapist is able to assess what is working and what is not and to change directions as often as necessary, until the client seems to have been helped by the intervention.

Practicing Creatively

Eminent writers and artists usually have a unique, identifiable style. The same could be said for effective clinicians. After all, there are limits on how far apprentices or disciples can go if they follow their mentors slavishly and cling to orthodoxy.

There is something to be said for technical competence — that is, the ability to apply the tools of one's trade successfully. However, being a truly gifted writer, artist, or therapist involves going far beyond what has been derived from others' work; it means having been able to integrate what has been done before into a personal and original vision, one that is ideally suited for that professional's unique assets and capabilities. As Yalom (1989, p. 36) explains, "If they are helpful to patients at all, ideological schools with their complex metaphysical edifices succeed because they assuage the *therapist's,* not the patient's, anxiety (and thus permit the therapist to face the anxiety of the therapeutic process). The more the therapist is able to tolerate the anxiety of not knowing, the less need is there for the therapist to embrace orthodoxy. The creative members of an orthodoxy, *any* orthodoxy, ultimately outgrow their disciplines."

I have been emphasizing what effective therapists have in common, but it is just as important to applaud their differences. The fact is that most of the world's best-known professionals, in our field or any other, are creative characters. They found a way to be most thoroughly themselves and invented a system or approach that encouraged them to be themselves. Just as clients get into trouble when they try to be somebody they are not, so too do therapists limit their powers when they attempt to be exactly like the mentors they most admire.

Compleat therapists have found their own voice. They are creative because they are not limited by what they have seen before. Each interaction with a client becomes a unique opportunity for creating a learning experience that has been individually and spontaneously designed, one that permits maximum flexibility and creativity in thinking and action.

Rogers (1986, pp. 48–49) captures the disadvantages of dogmatism as follows: "I believe that there is only one statement which can accurately apply to all theories—from the phlogiston theory to the theory of relativity, from the theory I will present to the one I hope will replace it in a decade—and that is that at the time of its formulation every theory contains an unknown (and perhaps at that point an unknowable) amount of error and mistaken inference. . . . To me this attitude is very important, for I am distressed at the manner in which small-caliber minds immediately accept a theory—almost any theory—as a dogma of truth. If theory could be seen for what it is—a fallible, changing attempt to construct a network of gossamer threads which will contain the solid facts—then a theory would serve as it should, as a stimulus to further creative thinking." These words apply as much to our own field as to any other.

Listening to Internal Voices

Minuchin (1986) traces the development of his own thinking in the voices of others that he hears constantly reverberating in his head. He believes (1986, p. 12) that his awareness of where the voices are leading him is what makes him most effective: "Clearly the voices I hear do not mean that everything is the same or that eclecticism is beautiful. The demands of a situation, and one's own possibilities and limitations, still operate selectively. Perhaps this is like the harmonic context of a melody. Within that context, a theme appears, is taken up by other voices, and can reappear in counterpoint or in inversion. Within the possibilities open to us, the best in us always learns from the best of others."

We are all like Minuchin in that we are the sum total of all the voices we have heard—the mentors and models and teachers who have demonstrated things we like. Our thinking often involves sorting out all of these voices, selecting those that speak to us most helpfully at a particular moment and then translating their words into a voice of our own.

A client remains stubbornly silent in response to what I believe was an especially insightful interpretation on my part. We stare at one another, waiting each other out, our minds whirring with activity. I hear a dissonant chorus of voices whispering to me and telling me what to do. In a matter of seconds, I try to identify all the different ways I have seen this situation handled by others.

My fourth-grade teacher would glower in a way that could melt lead, much less the puny resistance of a nine-year-old. I try a stern look, then hear echoes of *Not that!* and quickly mute my expresion to one of patient indulgence.

The whispers now become louder: *Wait him out. It's his responsibility to keep things going.* A moment of relief.

Then: *No, it's not. It's your job to keep things moving along. Isn't that what you're paid for?*

Yes! I must do something. But what?

Certainly there is no shortage of suggestions from the voices inside my head.

Interpret the silence as resistance.

Reframe the silence as a different form of nonverbal communication.

Stay with the silence. Respect what the client is saying.

Use humor to exaggerate the behavior.

Confront the client's game playing.

Stay calm. He just needs time to process what was said.

It is the last voice that speaks the loudest at this moment, so I pay attention to it. I even remember whose voice it is and where he was when he said it to me. It is my voice now. Because it fits with what I sense is happening. If the silence goes on more than a few minutes longer, I will think this through again and make a new decision about another voice to listen to, another voice that is part of my own.

As this example suggests, effective therapists give themselves many choices in the way they respond to clients. This makes it necessary to have an internal filing system that allows us to find what we are looking for. We could have the fastest computer in existence, one with virtually unlimited storage space and memory and with a collection of all the software we could find, but unless all this information is organized in such a way that it can be easily retrieved, it is useless.

Effective therapists not only know a lot and can do things well, but they have an organized system of information storage and retrieval that is highly efficient. They have the capacity to constantly upgrade their data, to refine their assumptions, and to restructure the way they view things based on new information and experiences. Thus the style of thinking adopted by almost all fine clinicians is remarkably similar. The best therapists have great capacity for empirical and logical analysis, yet they are also quite intuitive. They are flexible, multidimensional, and able to find patterns that most others cannot see. They are able to integrate the voices of their former teachers, and from this union of all that they know and sense and feel and understand, they are able to communicate clearly, sensitively, and perceptively.

CHAPTER SIX

What Therapists Actually Do with Clients That Makes a Difference

The therapist's ability to be helpful depends on more than his or her characteristic way of thinking and underlying personality qualities. There is also a consensus that some interventions are more likely than others to facilitate process goals. However, the relationship between therapeutic interventions and treatment outcomes is very complex.

As much as we would like to conceptualize therapy in terms of precise relationships between process variables and outcomes, what goes on between client and therapist is too complex, and its fabric too interconnected, to isolate single variables. That is why it has been so difficult to empirically substantiate that any single clinical action—whether it is the frequency of empathic responses or the duration of eye contact—consistently and universally makes a positive difference. Strupp (1989) believes that this search for effective technical skills has been disappointing because what is at issue is the meaning of these interventions to the client at a particular moment in time.

Another problem in identifying those behaviors, skills, and interventions that are most likely to be therapeutic is that clinicians differ so widely in their responses. Imagine, for example, a client statement such as the following: "I've been coming to you for a while, and whereas I appreciate all you have been trying to do for me, I don't feel any better; if anything, my symptoms are even worse! Do you see any hope for us continuing?"

Think about how you would respond to this client.

As is so often true in our profession, there is rarely a correct response or intervention that is called for, but rather a range of possible skills that may be employed. In the preceding example, any of these therapeutic reactions are possible:

1. *Reassurance.* "Sure. It just takes awhile. You need to be patient."
2. *Counterquestion.* "What changes have *you* noticed since we started working together?"
3. *Reflection.* "You seem to be feeling hopeless, as if nothing will help and you're doomed to spend the rest of your life like this."
4. *Acquiescence or paradoxical maneuver.* "Maybe you're right."
5. *Distraction from challenge.* "We can discuss that later. For now I wonder about what happened this week. You obviously feel distressed about something."
6. *Confrontation.* "I sense that you are challenging me to prove to you that this helps. It strikes me as a trap—if I agree, you will have an excuse to quit; if I disagree, you will accuse me of pressuring you into staying."

This, of course, is only a sampling of the possibilities and may not include your preferred response. The point is that there are many interventions that can be used appropriately in this or any other situation, making the task of cataloging effective therapeutic options very difficult. Nevertheless, I do believe that it is possible, and certainly useful, to summarize those therapist actions that are considered to be universally helpful across disciplines, theoretical orientations, and therapeutic styles.

A competent therapist, whether trained in social work, psychiatry, psychology, counseling, or nursing, whether working in crisis intervention or long-term relationships, whether operating psychodynamically, existentially, or behaviorally, is still going to be relying on similar actions that have been found to be helpful both clinically and empirically. For example, gestalt therapists, behavior therapists, and psychoanalysts use empathy, clarification, and interpretation similarly (Brunick and Schroeder, 1979; Sloane and others, 1975; Kazdin, 1986). Though the

various therapeutic approaches entail different theoretical constructs, they employ quite similar interventions.

The degree to which a clinician can consistently, accurately,
and skillfully apply therapeutic procedures and interventions
is of the utmost importance in producing positive outcomes
(White and Pollard, 1982; Beutler, Crago, and Arizmendi,
1986). Competence in therapy can be assessed according to the
degree of mastery the professional has reached in each of the
following clinical skill areas: selecting suitable clients, role induction, relationship building, interviewing, linguistic coaching, interpreting, confronting, handling resistance, focusing,
questioning, problem solving, setting limits, self-disclosure, and
dealing with endings. While hardly an exhaustive list of everything a competent therapist regularly does in sessions, these skills
are representative of clinical interventions that he or she must
master to function effectively. We will briefly discuss each of
them in the following paragraphs.

Selecting Suitable Clients

Since it is the client who contributes the most to successful
therapy outcomes in terms of a willingness to work sincerely
on personal issues, the most effective therapists are those who
can teach clients to optimize the benefits of their sessions. This
begins with selecting the best candidates for treatment: those
who are highly motivated, who have realistic expectations for
what they can accomplish, who are reasonably similar to the
therapist in terms of basic values, and whose style of psychological difficulty is amenable to psychotherapeutic intervention.

Effective therapists of all theoretical orientations are highly
skilled at selecting those clients who they believe they can help.
There is a mutual process of "checking each other out" that determines whether a good match exists between client and therapist personalities, values, styles, and expectations. Rarely, however, is this done explicitly. The therapist would hardly say
aloud, "I'm sorry, but I would prefer not to work with you.
You're too crazy/demanding/frustrating/manipulative. Let me
refer you to someone else." And just as infrequently would a

new client admit that "I don't think I like or trust you. You're too arrogant/cold/weird/withholding. So I won't be coming back."

Yet we do notice that a very similar process does occur in a much more subtle manner. No matter how broad our experience with a range of clientele may be, we find that occasionally, for no reason we can readily discern, a client drops out of treatment with no explanation given. We, of course, speculate on the reasons for this premature departure:

- "I probably cured her after this one session so there is no reason for her to come back."
- "She just took some time off to internalize all the provocative material we covered. She'll be back."
- "I'm too perceptive for her and she feels threatened at how well I could see through her."
- "She just doesn't have the motivation and commitment it takes to do well in therapy."

There are, of course, many other reasons the client does not return that may have to do with the way we handled things. But some of the time, clients drop out because they have decided they do not like us, for whatever reason. It could in fact be an excuse for keeping us at a distance if we get too close. But it can also be a matter of compatibility. Clients are looking for a therapist who they believe shares their basic values in life, who they perceive as attractive and trusting. And the fact is that we cannot be everything to everyone.

It is fascinating to listen to clients tell us why they quit treatment with other practitioners, what exactly they were shopping for in a helper. One therapist seemed too aloof and unapproachable. Another had this nervous habit of clearing his throat that was found distracting. One was too passive; another too active. Clients seem to know what they are looking for, and perhaps what is surprising is how many times the first encounter with a therapist turns out to be a beautiful match. This is a tribute to the effective therapist's adaptability — that is, his or her ability to reach so many different people with diverse backgrounds.

Still, some clients do not come back. And probably for valid reasons. Effective therapists accept this, acknowledging their inability to work with everyone all of the time and processing the feedback to help them become even more skilled in the future. They also recognize the importance of a good match. Therapists unconsciously discourage those clients they do not wish to work with — those they perceive as boring, who they do not believe they can help, or who present issues that are experienced as too personally threatening.

I am uncomfortable admitting that some clients get more from me than others, but I work harder if I feel more engaged. I am more accommodating in my scheduling and payment of fees. I am probably more understanding and patient. I know that some clients get to me more easily than others; I sometimes punish them by being withholding or being more confrontational than I need to be. So, naturally, I am less effective with them than I could be. Sometimes they might cancel an appointment and I am ashamed to admit that I feel relieved. I do not follow up with a phone call as quickly as I might with another client. All in all, I tell myself that these thankfully rare mismatches with me deserve someone who can be more compassionate than I can. They eventually leave dissatisfied unless we can work things through more honestly in sessions as to what is getting in the way for us.

If this is the worst part of me — that which feels most unprofessional — then one of the best parts of my work is when the client and I can deal with each other in an open manner and come to realize that someone else might be better for him or her. One case I can recall feeling especially good about involved a client who had the remarkable courage to confront me after a second session and tell me that she did not feel things were clicking between us. She did not think that I was "her kind of person." I was surprised at how nondefensive I felt, because usually I feel *very* threatened by this type of feedback, which I perceive as rejection. I shared with her how much I appreciated her honesty and openness. We were then able to put our heads together in the process of selecting another therapist who would be a better match for her. When she left, we both felt good about the interchange.

Rarely is this selection process so overt and direct. But the result is the same: we pick those clients we believe we can help, allowing the few others to drift away. Clients stay with therapists they believe can help them, and leave those who they perceive will not be helpful.

There are many other factors that play a part in each individual therapist's selection process. The effective psychoanalytic therapist is not going to agree to work with someone who wants only symptom relief but could care less about self-understanding. The cognitive therapist will stay with those clients who want to think more rationally. The existential therapist selects candidates who have the capacity and motivation to discover personal meaning in their lives in addition to having a high tolerance for ambiguity and suffering. The strategic therapist works best with clients who want quick symptomatic relief, without any interest in self-discovery. The gestalt therapist wants clients who are not so literal-minded, who will cooperate with spontaneous encounters. This is not to say that these or other specific treatment modalities cannot work with almost everyone. However, effective therapists know what they can do well and with what kind of clients. And they are good at screening out those who are likely to be poor risks.

Role Induction

The client walks in confused. He is uncomfortable with the lack of structure and the therapist's ambiguous role. There are a host of conflicting feelings and desires — to make a good impression, to present an accurate portrait of what has been going on, to defend himself against more pain, to be a "good client." And he experiences tremendous anxiety because of muddled expectations:

Where should I sit? What am I doing here? Where should I begin? What does she want from me? Is it okay to take my shoes off? Am I supposed to pay now or later? What is she going to do? What is she waiting for? Am I supposed to start?

Hello, my name is Dr. ____ . What can I do for you?"

"Um. Uh. Well, it . . . uh. I'm not sure." *What does she want to know? Should I just talk, or will she ask me questions? Should I give her*

*brief answers or long ones? Should I even tell her the truth? I hardly know
her.*

It is truly amazing that despite such humble beginnings, in a
matter of minutes this client will pick up what is expected of
him: to be as open and honest as possible and to be patient with
whatever unfolds. He will learn the rules of engagement—that
while the therapist *says* it does not matter what you talk about,
there are certain topics that seem more appropriate and certain
ways of talking about them that are most helpful. Before this
first session is over, the client will have a pretty good idea of
what to expect next time.

Clients stay in therapy longer and get more out of the experience when the roles of both client and therapist are clearly
delineated (Frank and others, 1978; Garfield, 1978; Richert,
1983). While the roles of the therapist are everchanging—from
consultant to compassionate listener to supportive friend to
authoritative expert to idealized parent—clients are helped to
take on the role of a cooperative, open, trusting participant. In
short, we are teaching clients to function optimally so that they
may get the most out of treatment and we might feel most comfortable (Chessick, 1982; Beitman, 1987).

Most of the ingredients of successful therapy are introduced
as the treatment first begins. Unless the therapist can recruit
the client's help, set up favorable expectations, establish realistic goals, structure a sound treatment plan, and initiate a productive working alliance, any further efforts will be doomed. Effective therapists are thus quite skilled at preparing the client for
what will follow in a way that maximizes receptivity and active
participation.

Inducting the neophyte into the role of a client involves several
important steps that are part of most intake procedures. If there
has ever been one area of consensus among practitioners of
different theoretical allegiances, it is that initial interviews should
have certain characteristics and goals beyond that of collecting
needed background information. Some of these components of
successful role induction have been proposed by Orne and
Wender (1968), Gottman and Lieblum (1974), Dyer and Vriend
(1977), and Beutler (1983); they include the following:

Providing a General Introduction to Psychotherapy. The client is usually given a general overview of the process — what it can and cannot do and what is likely to occur. Often this includes a discussion of ground rules related to fees, scheduling, and confidentiality.

Assessing the Client's Expectations. The client is questioned about what he or she believes will happen and is asked for perceptions of what the therapist will do. Through patience and probing, we eventually learn what the client really thinks about being in our office:

- "This feels awkward and humiliating and terribly uncomfortable."
- "I am probably crazy, and I am about to learn that my therapist will put me away forever."
- "There is no hope for the incurable condition I have contracted."
- "Talking to a complete stranger about my problems is ludicrous and a definite sign of weakness."
- "This is a sham and a rip-off, paying so much money for so little."
- "This probably won't work, and even if it did, it's too late."
- "After about two more sessions I'll be fixed for good, and I won't have to do much to make that happen."

Stating the Therapist's Expectations. With diplomacy and sensitivity, the therapist systematically eliminates each of the client's misperceptions about what therapy can do. The clinician provides an alternative reframing of therapy that is consistent with what he or she can actually deliver. For example, "I have no magic wand, but I do have some degree of expertise that will allow us together to explore what is going on and to help you find a way out."

The therapist also introduces the client to the behaviors expected of him or her. These might include some of the following:

- " . . . that you attend sessions regularly and promptly"
- " . . . that you give sufficient notice before canceling a session"

- "... that you agree to abide by office policies and pay bills according to our agreed-on schedule"
- "... that you not call my home number unless it is an absolute emergency"
- "... that you abstain from all alcohol and drug use while you are in treatment"
- "... that you accept primary responsibility for the content and direction our sessions take"
- "... that you try to be as open and honest with me as you can"
- "... that if things aren't going the way you like, you will take responsibility for making changes and letting me know what you need me to do differently"
- "... that you will give at least two weeks' notice before ending treatment so that we may work through unfinished issues between us"

Previewing Coming Attractions. The client is warned about, and prepared for, certain predictable occurrences that he or she may find uncomfortable. For example, the client is advised that he or she may feel some degree of discomfort throughout the experience, that at several junctures there may be a temptation to run away, and that these resistances are normal and even useful to moving forward. This is an especially important phase of the role induction process since it builds a certain amount of patience and indulgence into the client's expectations and gives the therapist latitude in helping the client process periods of discouragement and disillusionment.

Giving a Favorable Prognosis. The client wants and needs to hear that devoting this time, energy, and money is going to result in something tangible. While no guarantees can reasonably be offered, the therapist assures the client that what is ailing him or her is indeed workable, that it may take a while, but with sufficient motivation and hard work, the client will indeed experience significant improvement.

O'Hanlon and Weiner-Davis (1989) even recommend ending the first session by capitalizing on the client's positive expectations. They believe that rather than focusing exclusively on what is wrong with people — exploring and diagnosing their psychopathology — progress would be better served by asking clients to reflect on what is working for them. Thus they suggest asking clients to pay attention to all the positive or desirable things that occur during the week. For example, rather than spending time thinking about how often they argue, a couple can be directed to monitor everything about their relationship that they would like to nourish. A positive rather than a negative prognosis is therefore fostered.

Orienting the Client to New Behaviors. There are certain client behaviors that are essential for therapy to work. People who are used to externalizing their problems and blaming others for their suffering must give up these defenses in favor of alternative strategies that are consistent with the goals of therapy. Clients are taught to be more psychologically sophisticated, to be more introspective and analytic, and to begin looking at *their* role in creating difficulties for themselves.

There is usually a certain language and phraseology the therapist prefers the client to use that is representative of these new concepts. Thus the first or second time the client says "I need . . . " he or she may be asked to substitute "I want . . . ," or he or she may be encouraged to exchange "I won't" for "I can't." This sensitivity to language becomes one of the first signals for the new client that the rules of expression in therapy sessions are considerably different from conventional modes of thinking and talking.

Helping the Client Increase Tolerances. The client is helped to increase tolerances for certain experiences that will prove useful for the duration of the sessions. These will probably include expanding the client's range of vision — that is, increasing his or her willingness to consider new choices and possibilities. It also means increasing client tolerance for short-term suffering while rendering the prospect of long-term discomfort unacceptable. In other words, the client will have to tolerate the pain of the present symptomatology as well as disquieting confrontations with himself or herself until things can be worked through, but will no longer be forced to confront a mediocre future.

Tolerances for other states are also increased to make therapeutic work possible—so that the client can temporarily live with uncertainty, ambiguity, frustration, and other likely experiences that usually accompany this personal journey. This orientation to "nowhere land" starts the first time the client asks a direct question and is told "It's up to you," or when the session is ended with things left hanging in the air. Essentially, the client is quickly taught to increase his or her capacities for tolerating the unknown and the uncomfortable.

Obtaining a Commitment. When all else is said and done, the final and most important component of the role induction process is securing a commitment from the client that he or she will agree to the conditions of the contractual arrangement and work hard in the sessions. Without such a promise, the client will feel little investment in the therapy and little inclination to stay with the process when the going gets rough.

Kanfer and Schefft (1988) have argued that one of the most common reasons therapy fails is that the client is not sufficiently motivated; helping him or her develop a commitment to change is the central task of the clinician. They propose a variety of clinical skills and interventions that are often useful in (1) reducing the client's feelings of demoralization, (2) developing incentives for change in the clients, (3) obtaining a commitment from the client to participate in therapy, and (4) motivating the client to stay with treatment when the going gets rough.

It probably makes little difference exactly which techniques are used to accomplish these goals—whether the clinician prefers instituting positive imagery, recording progress in ways that make it easy to see changes, setting small but easily managed tasks, or using encouragement within the therapeutic alliance. Whatever particular style or approach is employed, the therapist must be successful in securing the client's commitment to follow through with the therapy process.

Relationship Building

Perhaps what makes therapists most effective is their ability to create trusting relationships with their clients. In the context of an alliance that consists of mutual affection, respect, openness, and excellent communication, there is much freedom for both participants. There is freedom for the client to explore unconscious motives, repressed experiences, and unexpressed feelings, and to experiment with new behaviors. But there is also freedom for the therapist to feel at ease and to make mistakes without jeopardizing future progress.

In a trusting relationship in which we have earned the client's confidence, we are not as pressured to perform perfectly. The most effective therapists are not those who know exactly what to do in every situation; rather they are those who have secured sufficient time and patience on the client's part to experiment until the most helpful combination of interventions is discovered.

It is not necessary to be right in every interpretation, to be on target with every confrontation, or to be successful with every therapeutic strategy, as long as we have the client's trust and indulgence. If he or she believes in our integrity and competence, then we have all the time we need to eliminate those approaches that do not work and select (or stumble on) those that will.

One practitioner — a counselor educator and therapist for over twenty years — believes that the essence of everything she does with her clients boils down to her skill and expertise in building productive relationships: "I suspect that those clients with whom I am most effective feel deeply heard and valued by me. If asked, I hope they would say I understand them on all levels and to the depth of their beings. When we are together, I 'fit' tightly around them. I work closely with them, picking up nuances and subtleties of thought and emotion. I catch their smallest feelings and ideas as they arise in the moment and stay present as these shift. I reflect the reality of their inner experience, thus giving them permission to move to deeper and deeper levels of awareness."

This counselor educator further describes what she considers to be the ultimate clinical skill as establishing a working relationship in a relatively short period of time. To do this the professional must exude a certain amount of charm, class, sincerity, tranquillity, magnetism, kindness, empathy, wisdom, and other characteristics that make someone attractive to others.

The effective therapist is seen as nurturing and safe, as someone who can truly be trusted with one's secrets, problems, and
well-being.

These qualities are communicated in the very being of the
therapist, in her energy and style, and also in her behavior. For
the effective therapist acts in ways that are designed to win confidence and instill a sense of trust. This is done by demonstrating one's skill as an attentive listener, without judgment or criticism. It is done in all the innumerable ways in which we show
our concern and caring.

Whereas Rogers (1957) was the primary spokesperson for the
healing benefits of communicating caring and positive regard
to the client, this skill (if it *is* a skill rather than a quality or
even more diffuse "way of being") is certainly part of the repertoire of every practitioner. Decker (1988) points out that most,
if not all, therapists act as caregivers of parental love. Even
though we accept financial remuneration in exchange for our
attention, clients feel a sense of genuine caring from us — or they
would not come back. (The notable exception to this point are
those clients who are so used to being in nonreciprocal, withholding relationships that they will tolerate aloofness, rejection,
and even disdain from their therapists because it is all they feel
they deserve.) Since, however, this discussion is concentrating
on the skills of the most effective therapists, we are justified in
saying that at least some degree of caring is evident in therapeutic
relationships.

It is not enough to care about our clients; most potent therapeutic effects result from the communication of this attitude
in such a way that the client can accept these positive feelings.
Indeed, perhaps the greatest skill is in communicating the positive regard in such a way that it is felt by the client, but is neither
misinterpreted as seductive nor seen as inauthentic. We are giving of ourselves — our loyalty, our undivided attention, our focused concentration. We hear, see, think, feel, and share what
we observe and sense.

The skills that are involved in this endeavor are initially taught
in graduate school: how to reflect feelings, offer support, and
demonstrate deep levels of empathy and understanding. Yet the

best therapists have integrated these interventions into their natural style of relating to others. They radiate a warm smile, soft eyes, and a presence that invites people to confide their deepest thoughts and feelings.

Effective therapists are also good at making adjustments when they sense that things are not going as well as they could. When they feel a client slipping away, they are able to quickly diagnose what they may be doing that is creating distance and what they might do to facilitate greater intimacy. They are able to adapt their style to the needs and requirements of each client, calculating when appropriate levels of familiarity or formality are needed.

Many clients report dissatisfaction with therapists they have seen because they were perceived as being either too loose or too rigid. A client confided his frustration with a therapist who was repeatedly asked for feedback and input on what had not been disclosed over a period of a dozen sessions, but instead encountered continued silence and passivity. The therapist refused to alter his style. Another client felt extremely uncomfortable with her therapist's informality and loose boundaries. She wanted more structure to feel safe and even expressed this to her therapist. But he, too, was unable or unwilling to change his style.

Some clients need more structure, others less. Some appreciate formality; others feel most comfortable in an informal setting. While generally we tend to keep those clients who are most like us in their basic interests and values, those therapists who are able to reach a broader population are those who are good at diagnosing just what a client needs to feel comfortable opening up — and then to deliver it.

Interviewing

There is both an art and a science to a therapeutic interview. Even the most nondirective of therapists finds it important to gather background information, relevant family and medical history, and other material that may prove helpful in understanding the context of the present situation. While the degree of structure used in initial interviews may vary from the most regimented of mental status examinations to a more open-ended discussion about what brought the client to the office, conducting such an exploration is a prerequisite for any treatment that would follow.

The best interviews are those that appear to be the most natural encounters, where the therapist is able to elicit volumes of information without resorting to an interrogative style. It is this low-key, nonthreatening approach that separates the veteran from the beginner. The effective therapist is able to encourage sharing, openness, and helpfulness on the part of the client through a host of ancillary skills such as open-ended questions, reflections of feeling, probes, and demonstrations of general interest. Like any great detective, the therapist is good at getting people to *want* to tell their story, complete with all the rich details that give it life and meaning.

There is probably remarkable consensus among practitioners of all theoretical orientations as to what information should be gathered during initial interviews. Such a list would include: a description of complaints and symptoms, the exact onset of problems and precipitating factors, previous history of emotional difficulties, a list of what has worked so far in coping with the problems, previous history of working with professional helpers, medical history including any medications being taken, previous or current illicit drug use, family constellations and history, current living situation, occupational and avocational activities, feelings about being in therapy, and reflections on how things are going so far. Marmor (1986) summarizes these various components; he suggests that careful history taking is intended to

1. Determine the onset of the symptoms (acute, chronic, precipitating factors)
2. Assess strengths the client brings to the sessions (intelligence, education, experience, support system)
3. Explore stresses in the client's life and capacities for dealing with them
4. Evaluate resources that are available in the client's world (quality of relationships, vocational and interpersonal skills, financial resources)

Rarely would this information be collected through rapid-fire "interrogation," although questionnaires are often provided to clients as part of an intake procedure. The skilled therapist is able to find out what has happened and what is currently going on in the client's life through the same process that is part of all good therapy — by being an attentive listener, by tracking themes and issues, by noting what is said and what is omitted, by providing a safe, secure environment conducive to sharing and exploration, and by clarifying things through questioning content and reflecting on underlying thoughts and feelings.

Linguistic Coaching

Since therapy is an act of communication, much of what takes place is centered around the content and structure of linguistic processes. In a sense, therapists function as language coaches who listen carefully to what is communicated and how it is expressed. Much of the time, the messages contain distortions, exaggerations, overgeneralizations, erroneous assumptions, and inconsistencies that can be altered to represent more accurate aspects of reality or healthfulness.

Whereas it is obvious the way linguistic philosophers such as Ludwig Wittgenstein would devote considerable attention to the differential meaning of expressive language, there is also a rich heritage of these methods evident in much of therapeutic work. With the growing popularity of cognitive-based therapy and neurolinguistic programming, most practitioners have become quite adept at monitoring and shaping client language patterns.

The rational-emotive therapist believes that by learning to talk to yourself differently, you will subsequently think and feel differently. The neurolinguistic therapist is also concerned with correcting distortions of reality implied in verbal communication. The gestalt therapist finds it helpful to encourage clients to adopt the language of self-responsibility. And since it is the primary tool with which to influence the client, all practitioners are concerned with the precise and constructive application of language.

There are, for example, a number of ways in which therapists apply linguistic coaching skills in their work:

1. *Correcting distortions or exaggerations of reality.* "When you say you have *never* been successful in *anything* you have ever tried, I presume you are speaking only about your most recent attempt to find a date."
2. *Pointing out errors in logic.* "Perhaps I'm missing something here, but you said that *your* suffering is caused by what *others* have said to you?"
3. *Clarifying ambiguous referents.* "When you speak of people who should be more sensitive to others' feelings, what you mean is that your husband could be more attuned to *your* feelings."
4. *Helping clients to express more completely and fully the exact nature of their internal experiences.* "What is it like for you to feel out of control?"
5. *Teaching clients to avoid the use of certain words, phrases, and expressions that can be considered counterproductive.* "I wonder if you wouldn't mind repeating what you just said, but this time substitute *I want* for *I need, I won't* for *I can't,* and *I prefer* for *I must.*"
6. *Encouraging clients to use the language of self-responsibility.* "You have been talking at length about how everyone feels in this group. You might try using the pronoun *I* to speak only for yourself."
7. *Pinning down responses that are evasive.* "You keep saying *maybe, probably,* and *I don't know.* Take a wild guess and tell me what you think might happen."
8. *Confronting sexism, racism, class prejudice, and other forms of bias to facilitate a deeper understanding of their impact on others.* "I notice you use derogatory terms whenever you refer to women—expressions like *bitch, my old lady,* and *weaker sex.* Let's look at what effects that might be having on some of your relationships."

As therapists, we must be sensitive to our clients' use of language. But we not only need to be skilled at logical analyses of words and their meanings; we should be experts at our own use of language. Since it is our job to offer a reality that, if not more objective, is at least healthier than our clients', words and gestures are the principal means available to us in our efforts to clarify what we hear and offer interpretations regarding possible meanings.

Interpreting

Interpretation is the basis for much of our therapeutic work, since it is our job to draw together client material into statements of possible significance. It is an attempt to represent reality accurately in language that may be understood. As such, it is an aesthetic venture rather than an assertion of a truth or falsehood that cannot be verified (Spence, 1982). Like any work of art, it must be beautifully conveyed, arrest attention, and be a stimulus for discovering personal meaning. It is proposed as a hypothesis, a possibility of what may be, subject to the ways it is internalized by the listener.

Interpretation is the act of assigning meaning or causality to behavior or experience (Beitman, 1987). When we increase clients' awareness of patterns in their lives, they can no longer get away with acting in self-defeating ways without realizing what they are doing and why. A case in point is demonstrated by Nina and Nicholas, a couple who are especially wrathful in their conflicts with one another. The marital therapy that takes place consists of the clinician playing referee to stop them from doing irreparable damage to one another in their reciprocal attacks. The therapist interpreted a pattern she had observed again and again in which each partner would take turns sparking an argument during times of relative tranquillity. The other spouse would then take on the role of abused victim and milk the part to the hilt — until it became tiresome, when according to some unspoken agreement, they would switch roles of antagonist and defender. This carefully choreographed production was, of course, reminiscent of the behavior they had each seen modeled by their own parents at home. They had each auditioned candidates for the role of spouse over a long period of time until they found a suitable match.

It never became necessary to resort to an intrusive, strategic intervention — paradoxical, directive, or otherwise. The awareness of their pattern became embarrassing enough that they

could no longer engage in ridiculous behavior without one of
them realizing what they were doing and refusing to continue
playing out the same script.

Family therapists — especially those who practice brief therapy, such as Fisch, Weakland, and Segal (1982), Budman and
Gurman (1988), and Haley (1990) — see their essential mission
of affecting cures within a half-dozen sessions as altering the
client's perception of his or her presenting complaint. This
reframing is accomplished mostly through the presentation of
an alternative interpretation of the problem in such a way that
it may be more easily solved. Thus Weiner-Davis (1990) describes the case of a discouraged and demoralized single woman
who had all but given up male companionship because of an
image of herself as a loser. The therapist reinterpreted the issue in terms that were not only easier to work with, but in a
way that reduced the client's sense of hopelessness — that the client
needed to construct a more effective "self-marketing" strategy.

These sorts of interpretations, while the antithesis of traditional psychoanalytic interventions, nevertheless demonstrate
the clinician's potential to suggest alternative realities that the
client may find helpful. Bernstein (1965) summarized other uses
of interpretation as a means to: facilitate insight, provide solutions, alleviate anxiety, inhibit acting out, improve communication, handle resistance, offer support, increase awareness, and
infer causes of action. In each of these cases, the therapist seeks
to label or explain phenomena in order to make them both understood and manageable (Dollard and Auld, 1959).

It does not really matter what type of interpretation is offered
to the client — be it an existential, psychoanalytic, or cognitive-
behavioral formulation. As long as it is a convincing, relatively
comprehensible explanation of the source of conflicts, the client
will find the therapist to be both reassuring and helpful (Garfield,
1980).

So we are dealing with style here rather than content. The
client comes in and presents himself as agitated and anxious.
He does not sleep well, waking up almost every hour of the night.
In addition, he reports he has no goals in life, or anything in
particular to look forward to. He is looking, desperately seek-

ing, some explanation for this disturbing state of affairs. He does not care where it comes from — only that it reassures him that he is going to be all right, that he is not in fact falling apart.

One interpretation of his situation that could easily be proposed is that the meaninglessness he is experiencing in his life, the lack of purpose and direction, is keeping him up all night. The symptoms are creating the necessary discomfort to motivate action. They are his body's way of getting and keeping his attention until he takes care of unfinished business. If the therapist presents it with authority and eloquence, this interpretation may offer some comfort and understanding. The client would probably feel less anxious immediately, just from learning that this is a natural and even a necessary situation for him to live through. This interpretation would be effective because it makes sense to him. It is not so important to him *what* the explanation is as much as that there *is* an explanation for what is bothering him.

Effective therapists of all theoretical persuasions would make use of similar interpretive procedures — that is, giving meaning, even if it is only a working hypothesis, to a situation that seems frightening and hopeless. With the preceding client, I offered just such an interpretation of his plight, quite proud of myself all the while — thinking I had (1) tied together most of the threads of his story, (2) proposed an idea that seemed logical and intellectually sound, and (3) explained the theory in a highly impassioned and convincing manner designed to recruit his support. He would, however, have no part of it. Although, he admitted, the idea did have some merit, it did not "feel right" to him. He was quick to reassure me that he could see how I might think that, and perhaps it was true — but it did not seem to help him much.

I responded by offering another interpretation that I thought he would accept until he was ready or able to face some other issues. I recalled that the frequent waking problems had started gradually when he turned thirty, and they had been getting steadily worse. My interpretation of his situation was rather simple: I told him that most men over thirty begin to experience decreasing bladder capacity, which leads to the necessity of more frequent urination in the middle of the night. Now whether this is really what is going on with him or not is beside the point. The point is that this explanation made perfect sense to him (much to *my* surprise). He felt more relaxed, more hopeful, and relieved enough to begin to explore the other issues in his life.

This case illustrates how interpretations can be used to reduce client anxiety. However, the primary purpose of this intervention is to promote insight and self-awareness, a process that often involves a certain amount of discomfort. Pope (1977) has observed that interpretation is an especially difficult skill to master since it is not only helpful; it can also be quite dangerous.

The client will not accept interpretations that are too deep, and those that are especially threatening will provoke greater resistance and defensiveness. Superficial and shallow interpretations, on the other hand, can be perceived at best as a waste of time, and at worst can be seen as evidence the therapist does not really understand what the client is communicating.

The worst kind of interpretations are those that appear pejorative, denigrating, or accusatory. Strupp (1989) believes that often a client's negative reactions are not due to resistance or pathology, but the natural defensiveness to perceived attacks: the client feels hurt and rejected. Here are a few examples of how interpretations can be framed negatively or positively. One alternative would be to say, "You seem to be acting out toward your wife just as you did toward your mother." But consider this version: "There seem to be some similarities between your relationships with your wife and mother." Or, for another example, "You feel helpless and trapped, but don't seem to want to do anything to change." The following version would have a much more positive effect: "There's a part of you that really wants to get better, and yet another part of you that likes things the way they are."

The principal task, then, for therapists is to offer opinions that are plausible to the client as well as insightful, without creating further resistance. Strupp advises that interpretations are most helpful when the therapist shows empathy, metacommunicates about the process without being specifically critical, and frames interventions carefully, diplomatically, and positively.

Confronting

While it is indeed counterproductive to create undue stress through the use of misguided interventions, there is an appropriate time and place for exacerbating the client's dissonance. Beutler (1986) believes this to be the hallmark of all effective therapy.

The purpose of confrontation is to help the client face discrepancies between aspects of his or her behavior and espoused attitudes, values, and goals (Dyer and Vriend, 1975). This may include pointing out differences between:

1. *What was said earlier and what is being said now.* "Earlier you mentioned that growing up in your home was so calm and pleasant, yet you are relating one instance after another in which things actually sound quite conflicted and stressful."
2. *What was verbalized versus what was actually done.* "You said finding a new job is so important to you, yet you have been so reluctant to go out on any interviews."
3. *What is implied in one aspect of communication (nonverbal communication, expressions of feeling, intellectual responses, and so on) but contradicted in another.* "You report feeling comfortable right now and free of any concerns, yet you appear rigid, tense, and controlled. Your speech is tight, your knuckles are white, and you are unable to meet my eyes."

In each of these examples, or any confrontation, the therapist seeks to induce higher levels of dissonance in the client by forcing him or her to examine inconsistencies. When discomfort has been increased to uncomfortable but manageable limits, several things begin to happen: the client lets go of previous strategies that are clearly not working, the disequilibrium motivates a search for something else that will reduce discomfort, and the disorientation leads to a degree of experimentation with other alternatives that were previously unacceptable.

Dysfunctional behavior is, in many ways, the avoidance of issues and conflicts that will not go away by themselves. Clients develop defenses and adaptive mechanisms to protect them from dealing with painful material. Effective therapists use direct or indirect confrontation as the primary means of helping clients face the problems they have been avoiding. Garfield (1986, pp. 153–154) believes the common factor in all approaches "appears to be that the client in some way is confronted with the negative situation and learns that he can face it without any catastrophic consequences."

Handling Resistance

One of the first paradoxes confronted by a beginning therapist is that whereas clients universally claim they wish to change, there is a part of them that would prefer that things stay just the way they are. We have learned that this phenomenon holds true for a number of reasons: fear of the unknown; reluctance to accept responsibility; repression, denial, or other defenses to keep the unconscious buried; reactions to perceived threat; anger or resentment toward the therapist for some perceived injustice; transference acting out; self-defeating personality style; sense of hopelessness; and so on. In fact, there are so many reasons why resistance occurs that it is a wonder anyone changes at all!

Nevertheless, effective therapists are highly skilled at dealing with client reluctance, respecting the messages it conveys, and using the conflict for the purposes of learning and growth. Imagine, for instance, how you would respond to a client you have been seeing for some time who does any of the following:

- consistently comes five to ten minutes late to every session
- cancels or reschedules sessions on a regular basis
- becomes unduly argumentative over apparently insignificant points
- remains silent for lengthy periods of time
- denies the existence of conflicts that appear evident
- agrees with almost everything you say
- reports not thinking about the content of therapy between sessions
- changes the subject whenever certain matters arise
- indulges in incessant chatter, filling the time with long-winded, rambling monologues

- maintains feelings of abject hopelessness in the face of any and all interventions
- expresses anger and hostility without provocation
- fervently denies the presence of *any* feelings toward you

Decker (1988) reminds us of the value that psychoanalytic thinking has brought to the understanding and management of the behaviors just listed. The analyst has taught us that opposition to treatment is not only to be expected in a therapeutic encounter, but is viewed as a healthy way of pacing progress until the ego is strong enough to deal with threatening material. As such, resistance is respected as a legitimate, albeit indirect form of communication. Once recognized, in all its many guises, it can be brought to the client's attention. Its origins, meanings, and motives are further explored, including its functional values.

Effective therapists have adopted a nonadversarial attitude toward client resistance so as to minimize feelings of being personally attacked as well as being able to neutralize the negative energy. To borrow a metaphor from the martial arts such as T'ai Chi, sparring is not seen as a match between opponents but rather as an encounter between partners. The object of this exercise is to maintain one's own sense of balance in the presence of someone else who is trying to maintain his or her own balance in the same space that you are occupying. When we are attacked by an opponent who is pushing against us, the most advantageous way to counter it is *not* by pushing back; rather, it is to absorb the force, neutralizing it by not presenting any surface for him or her to push against. The act of T'ai Chi sparring, like that of resistance in therapy, consists of recognizing that one's partner is defending or attacking, and dissipating the force of aggressive energy by shifting one's position and thereby causing him or her to miss the target.

Some therapists are able to work through therapeutic resistance in such a way that they are able to minimize their own sense of frustration at the same time that they are able to help clients reach a point of futility where they are willing and ready to abandon their self-defeating ploys. The literature is full of advice, techniques, and strategies for dealing with resistance, including everything from giving more of the self or less, to being more open or less revealing, to setting stricter boundaries or looser ones, to confronting the symptoms or exaggerating them. The most important variables seem to include: (1) staying calm internally; (2) being more inventive, creative, and flexible; (3) remaining patient; (4) respecting what the resistance is saying; (5) recognizing and avoiding traps that are intended to derail progress; (6) continuing to be caring and accepting toward the person while not tolerating unacceptable behavior; (7) interpreting what is occurring and helping the client to see his or her covert actions and underlying motives; (8) reassuring the client that this is a normal reaction, considering the circumstances; and (9) admitting your own role and responsibility in exacerbating the situation.

Many diverse writers, including Langs (1981), Goldfried, (1982a), Masterson (1983), and Ellis (1985), have felt that the greatest source of resistance in therapy comes not from the client but from the therapist. When unresolved issues are triggered in sessions, or when the clinician has a low frustration tolerance or a high need for approval, the most minor resistance can escalate into major impediments to progress. Effective therapists try hard to be aware of the source of process difficulties, whether they emanate from the client or from themselves. They are both committed to and expert at confronting their own resistance to looking at unresolved issues as these are ignited by client struggles.

Focusing

One interesting attempt to synthesize the ingredients common to all effective therapies was undertaken by Fuhriman, Paul, and Burlingame (1986) in their efforts to operate a university counseling center more efficiently. Confronted with a hopelessly unwieldy waiting list of prospective clients, the authors sought to develop a time-limited eclectic model that would employ the best features of all therapies. They identified *focusing* as one of the major mechanisms of change that is promoted through therapist interventions.

Focusing consists of offering some degree of structure to the therapeutic endeavor — that is, helping a client who is confused, frustrated, and imprecise in articulating what is wrong to center on areas that are likely to be most helpful. Focusing can involve any of the following:

1. *The act of making elusive, abstract, and ambiguous verbalizations more specific and concrete.* "So when you say you are unhappy, what you mean is that your closest relationships feel impoverished and devoid of intimacy."
2. *Reframing the client's conception of the problem as a treatment hypothesis that can be more realistically attained.* "When you say you want me to make your wife understand your position, what you really mean is that I should help *you* to become more effective in getting across your ideas in a way that your wife can hear them."
3. *When the client rambles incessantly, the therapist keeps the progress and development of a session centered around a particular theme.* "I notice that you have been talking about everything other than what originally brought you here."
4. *When the client begins to externalize problems and fixate on others as the cause of his or her suffering, the therapist focuses attention back on the client.* "You keep relating the source of your problems as the fault of your parents, your boss, and plain bad luck. In what ways are *you* responsible for your present plight?"

There is considerable variation in the degree of importance that different therapists would place on the value of focusing. Some practitioners, especially those working under the pressures of a time-limited model, would see focusing interventions as imperative to keep therapy proceeding in an efficient manner. Yet even those who prefer to allow clients to structure and lead the sessions at their own pace have developed subtle means to focus progress in areas that are likely to be most fruitful. When the client-centered therapist reflects feelings, she makes a choice as to which client statement is most worthy of attention and which feeling seems most important. When the psychoanalytic therapist asks about a dream, he is focusing attention on what he considers to be the most productive path. All effective therapists similarly take some degree of control in helping sessions flow smoothly and efficiently.

Questioning

Asking questions is the most direct way of eliciting information. Questioning is also helpful as a focusing tool, to provide a structure for sharing and exploration, in creating a transition to new subjects, and in identifying meaningful therapeutic content (Long, Paradise, and Long, 1981). And yet, when awkwardly worded, questioning cuts off communication, puts the client on the defensive, creates dependencies, and leads to the expectation that the therapist will continue to assume primary responsibility for session flow. It can also limit exploration in other areas and lead the client to feed answers the therapist wants to hear (Gazda and others, 1977).

Decker (1988) has explained that many therapists use questioning so routinely that they never stop to consider that they may be acting out their own pathology rather than actually trying to help the client. This can include our voyeurism in wanting to know certain private facts for our own titillation, our narcissism in wanting to elevate ourselves by asking difficult questions that the client cannot answer, and our sadism in harassing the client with painful queries.

Effective therapists know when they should or should not question clients, and when they are only attempting to meet their own needs. There are times when it is crucial to provide structure, elicit information, or facilitate exploration in a specific area. And there are times when the client is best left to flounder a bit and, with support, be allowed to work things out for himself or herself.

Like most interventions, the best questions are generally ambiguous and open-ended so that the way the client chooses to interpret them reveals as much as the answers that are supplied. Most clinicians avoid asking "why" questions since the client rarely knows why anything happens the way it does; instead they use inquiries to stimulate introspection or discussion. Common examples include:

- "What meaning does this have for you?"
- "What will you do with this insight?"
- "How are you feeling about what I just said?"
- "How are you going to proceed next?"
- "How does this seem familiar to you?"

In most cases, questioning is designed to help the client to clarify themes, synthesize issues, and explore areas that appear confusing. While extremely difficult to do without being intrusive or abusive, questioning is among the most direct means of eliciting important information in specific areas.

Problem Solving

As uncomfortable as most of us are with being identified as problem solvers — preferring instead to replace *problem* with *concern,* which does not imply that there is a single solution — we do attempt to resolve situations that seen unresolvable. We do this mostly by teaching clients to be their own problem solvers, to become aware of feelings and factors, to reason through the consequences of certain actions, to take steps likely to reach their desired goals. But therapists are also highly skilled at seeing the obvious that others have missed and at distilling the essence of complex situations. Often this involves going through an internal dialogue — or even leading the client through such a process — in which we ask things like:

- "What *is* the actual problem?"
- "What is the desired goal?"
- "What options are available for realizing that goal?"
- "Which of these alternatives are likely to be most useful?"
- "What is a course of action that can be used to implement this plan?"
- "To what extent have the desired goals been met?"

Most of us learned to operate in a problem-solving framework in graduate school. Often with considerable resistance, we conformed to the prescribed standards of doing research, writing a paper or thesis, or completing all the paperwork at internship sites. Therapy, of course, does not proceed in an organized, predictable manner — despite what insurance companies seem to expect when they mandate treatment plans that specify the exact diagnosis and course of intervention to be followed.

Many of the strategic practitioners, such as Bandler and Grinder (1975), Fisch, Weakland, and Segal (1982), Madanes (1981), Haley (1984), and de Shazer (1988), epitomize the effective use of problem-solving strategies in therapy. While some practitioners may have some difficulty embracing these brief therapists' assumptions that insight is irrelevant, or that there is no such thing as resistance, they do offer some marvelously inventive techniques that have great appeal. Some of these interventions, likened to a skeleton key or broad-based antibiotic, work with most clients most of the time. For example, de Shazer (1985) and O'Hanlon and Weiner-Davis (1989) describe the "basic miracle question," in which the client is asked to go into the future to a time when his or her problems have been resolved. "What, then, did you do to fix them?", the client is next asked. The response, of course, provides the key to which path is likely to be most effective. Another popular problem-solving task is the "exception question" — clients are simply asked to describe those times when their problems do *not* occur. For instance, parents complaining of a belligerent and surly adolescent are asked to focus on those times when he is cooperative and loving. With these examples, or with other strategic interventions such as "reframing," "prescribing the symptoms," or "forcing the spontaneous," the clinician works as a problem solver who is trying to find satisfactory solutions.

While strategic and other action-oriented or directive practitioners use problem-solving skills in quite direct ways, those who work in a more indirect, insightful style also make use of such methodologies, albeit in a looser framework that nevertheless cuts through to the essence of a client's difficulty. A psychiatrist who follows many of the tenets of structuralism and ego psychology describes what he considers to be the core of how he operates as a therapist. He supplies the following example as representative of what makes him most effective as a helper:

A professional woman had remarried and was living at what had been her home in the country. She and her husband, who earned less than she did, had one car that he drove most of the time, leaving her stranded whenever he was gone evenings and weekends. She complained to me: "I can never go anywhere." I immediately replied, "Why don't you buy your own car?" She looked puzzled for a minute, wondering to herself before she answered me, "I don't know." Later that day she bought a new car.

So what happened? I made a difference, but why, how, and what for? Maybe I missed the point; what she really wanted to deal with was her deep loneliness, her demands for nurturance from a mother, husband, therapist who were never "present." Maybe she missed the point, running away once again from facing that pain. Maybe she needed my permission to do her own thing, to get out on her own and explore the world. Maybe she just wanted to please me, to show some improvement that would make me feel better. Maybe she was truly a stranger to her own autonomy.

I think that understanding this interaction requires observation of what she did with the car and with isomorphs of the car. (We surely would not want a "flight or drive into health," one of those horrible transference cures, at this point. We never want to quit when we are on a roll, which has led one skeptic to write that a successful therapy is terminated at a point of mutual boredom.) These observations provide a context of meanings that cannot be derived from an analysis of this one chunk of behavior. Or so goes my myth!

This psychiatrist, as most of us would feel similarly, would bristle at the prospect of being called a problem solver, or even a derivative of that label such as a teacher of problem-solving skills. Yet our problem-solving abilities allow us to proceed

in ways that are somewhat organized, sequential, and hierar-
chical. We help clients to slowly build on what they already
know, understand, and can do. We do this by constantly assessing (even unconsciously and intuitively): Where have we
been? Where are we now? Where are we headed?

Setting Limits

It is a paradox that within an atmosphere of maximum permissiveness there is also the enforcement of certain inviolate
rules. Indeed the effective therapist must maintain a delicate
balance between permitting experimentation and encouraging
the acting out of spontaneous feelings and desires on the one
hand and setting limits as to appropriate conduct within the contractual relationship on the other.

An analytic therapist, who is comfortable deferring completely
to the client with regard to the selection of content and direction
in sessions, nevertheless feels that one of the most important
skills she has mastered is the establishment of clearly defined
limits in the therapeutic relationship: "I set firm boundaries with
my clients and I believe this is crucial to helping them assume
greater responsibility in their lives. They understand that if they
work with me they have to make a commitment to come regularly
and punctually. By setting parameters such as this, and confronting clients when there are attempts to be manipulative, I am
helping them to develop coping skills within reasonable limits."

This very point is illustrated in the case of a rather timid,
passive, depressed woman with a long history of hurting herself when she felt out of control. Her therapist tolerated a great
deal of flexibility in the way they spent their time together, sometimes sitting silently for a whole session, other times patiently
repeating encouragement a dozen times until she could hear the
words. However, it was not only the permissiveness and acceptance of the client that aided her recovery: "I believe the most
important thing that I did for her was to let her know quite
clearly what was okay and what was not. She would test me
continuously. Calls at home. Threats of self-mutilation. One
game after another. It was when I intervened in a firm man-

ner, telling her it was not okay for her to act in dangerous and irresponsible ways, that she regained her control. I learned in my training many years ago that I should be unconditionally accepting, yet over the years I have since modified my view to accept conditionally certain behaviors that could be quite destructive."

Kroll (1988) has pointed out in his work with borderline clients that the consummate therapist skill necessary to promote growth is mastering the art of engagement. This would in fact be true of work with any person. We attempt to maintain an optimal distance that allows us to get close, but not too close: "I am reminded of a passage in Hemingway's *The Sun Also Rises* in which a duel between the matador and bull is described. There is a proper distance between the protagonists within which the interaction most meaningfully occurs. If the matador is too concerned with his own safety, he maintains too great a distance between himself and the bull, so that little engagement occurs. If the matador works too closely to the bull and is too reckless, either because of concern for his own image or because of ignorance of the risks involved, then he is likely to be gored." (Kroll, 1988, p. 101).

With the flair of a bullfighter (although we are hardly encountering an adversary), a therapist works hard to maintain boundaries and limits that are both safe and yet within effective range to make contact. These parameters are established with regard to roles, expected behaviors, and limits to protect both participants. The tremendous skill involved in creating and maintaining these boundaries allows the therapist to become intensely intimate with a person, but without jeopardizing his or her own welfare or that of the vulnerable client.

With clients who are manipulative, narcissistic, or exploitative, or who show borderline or hysterical features, the therapist must work extra carefully to set limits without creating feelings of alienation. The problem is, then, to be careful without being withholding, to be warm without being seductive, to be supportive without fostering dependencies, to be firm without being punitive, to be compassionate without getting sucked into the client's destructive patterns.

There is a moment forever frozen in my mind when I stood poised with my hand on the phone and a client was deciding whether to walk out of the office or not. She was an adolescent who had just threatened suicide, after which I asked her to promise she would not hurt herself before our next session. She refused. I told her that she then left me little choice but to call her parents and inform them of her precarious state. She became enraged: "How dare you call my parents without my permission! What about the promise you made to keep our talks confidential?"

"You are correct. I would be breaking confidentiality. But if you walk out the door without being able to make a promise you won't hurt yourself, you are telling me by your behavior to call your parents because you are so out of control."

She looked at me, one foot out the open door, and she *knew* I would do it. We had agreed long ago there were boundaries that had to be maintained. And if she crossed the line of responsible conduct, then I would have to cross another line to safeguard her welfare. This is, of course, standard operating procedure. Yet, it takes a great deal of skill to set limits without jeopardizing the trust in the alliance.

The effective therapist has discovered a way that he or she can become truly engaged with even the most destructive of clients, but without collapsing those barriers that help provide structure and limits when they are needed. By way of contrast, there are those relatively inexperienced and unwary clinicians who proceed blithely, allowing themselves to be manipulated or seduced wherever the client's pathology may lead. Or there are those who are so fearful of even the controlled closeness of a rigidly structured therapy process that they become completely detached and disengaged from any authentic connection with the client whatsoever. Balance, of course, is the key to be mastered—being permissive enough to encourage free and spontaneous expression but also sufficiently restrictive of those behaviors and ploys that are ultimately self-defeating.

These include:

1. Playing mind games to discredit or devalue the therapist
2. Testing limits of tolerance surrounding missed or late appointments, frantic calls at home, delinquent payments

3. Hostile, angry, or dramatic outbursts intended to elicit some response
4. Threats of suicide, self-mutilation, or self-destructive acts
5. Coming to sessions under the influence of some mind-altering substance
6. Attempts at emotional or sexual seduction to knock the therapist off a pedestal

There is indeed tremendous skill required to manage each of these relatively common manifestations of disturbed behavior. This involves not only what is said and done with the client to neutralize the unacceptable behavior, but also what we tell ourselves in order to stay relatively clear and calm inside.

Self-Disclosure

There is no doubt that self-disclosure is probably the single most difficult therapist skill to use appropriately and judiciously. The therapist's revealing of self during sessions can be tremendously useful as a way to encourage a strong identification and mutual bond with the client. It is a way to model effective behaviors, to share instructive anecdotes, and to close the perceived distance between client and therapist, thereby facilitating greater trust and openness. Therapist self-disclosure begets client self-disclosure.

One resistant adolescent was even more surly than I am accustomed to — even for a withdrawn, angry boy referred by his parents against his will. Since his mother insisted that he come for a few months because she was tired of seeing him mope around the house in a deep funk, we each felt stuck with one another. All my usual ways of attempting to engage him proved futile; each well-intended reflection of his feelings or well-meaning question about things I knew he was interested in were met only with scornful grunts.

After the first month, about all I got out of him was that he was angry and depressed because his girlfriend had ended their relationship six months earlier and she refused to consider a reconciliation. He just wished to be left alone by everybody — by his teachers, his sisters, his parents, and especially by me.

We were reduced to spending our time playing gin rummy and poker, but it seemed like we were both biding our time, waiting for the two months to end so we could satisfy his parents.

It was stating that very synopsis of our mutual plight that finally got his attention. I told him how silly I felt talking to myself with him as a critical audience. I shared my frustration and impotence in trying to reach him in any way. Without my quite being aware of it, other feelings began to pour out of me, especially about how I could feel his pain, not as *his,* but as my own. Just as if it had happened last week, I began to relate my own traumatic breakup with a girlfriend in college — one that left me broken and despondent for months and months. In fact, even now after twenty years, I can still feel the pain.

As my eyes started to mist up a bit, a great wracking sob from the young man interrupted my story. The words and tears that had been stored inside him for so long finally flowed out. We had made contact.

Therapists who are highly skilled at self-disclosure are able to reveal themselves freely yet sparingly. They are not afraid to show their humanness, but do so without taking the focus off the client for any great length of time. The key criterion in knowing when to use this skill seems to be to use it only when there is an obvious reason why another intervention (which keeps the focus on the client) cannot work just as well.

There are many practitioners who prefer not to reveal themselves with clients for any number of reasons, most notably that it can lead to self-indulgence. And indeed there are some therapists who are so narcissistic and self-involved that they define their work primarily in terms of telling stories about themselves. This, hopefully, is the exception, not the rule. But so many of the mentors we consider to be most influential to our development are people who revealed themselves to us in a uniquely personal way — and we appreciated those gifts as much as we did their knowledge.

Whitaker (1986, p. 90) makes the very interesting point that the reason Freud created such strong prohibitions against therapists revealing themselves to their clients was not only because it can lead to unnecessary self-indulgence or confuse the transference, but because it makes the clinician more vulnerable. He or she can be seen as the patient. And of course the therapist's privacy is at stake; anything said in an interview is public information. Self-disclosure can also create a number of problems when it is employed at inopportune moments or when it is used excessively. There are, in fact, some practitioners who seemed to enter the field so they can have a captive audience to talk about themselves to. And even otherwise effective practitioners can see their well-intended self-disclosure backfire before their eyes.

During the same period in which I found that revealing my own story to the resistant boy worked wonders in cementing a bond between us, I decided to try a similar intervention with another case I felt stuck with. While I should have known that we tend to get into trouble whenever we attempt to impose a structure on a client, rather than allowing the exact situation to dictate the best match of strategy, I was riding high on my previous success. "Why," I reasoned, "shouldn't revealing myself more often help in other cases as well?"

Indeed, on the surface things appeared to be similar to the other situation, since the case involved a young woman who was mostly mute in sessions and refused to reveal real feelings about her life. When I pressed her to share feelings she may have toward me after spending a dozen hours together, she replied smugly that she did not think about me one way or the other. To her, I was just part of the furniture.

It was *because* I lost sight of my objective—to help her open up at her own pace, not my own—that I let my own needs get in the way. In anger and exasperation I used self-disclosure as a weapon (although at the time I reasoned that I was trying to push her to respond in some way, *any* way). I shared with her my own feelings that I felt abused and manipulated, that I thought she was playing games with me—and herself.

To my initial satisfaction, my remarks struck home. She *did* react! But in a way I hardly expected: "It takes me a long time to trust someone. I have been hurt so many times before. Where do you get off telling me that I'm not okay because I don't respond the way you want me to? You have just proven to me that I can't even *pay* someone to be cordial to me. While I do accept some responsibility for this mess, you are way out of line. I think it's best if I find someone else who can be a little more understanding."

After we both licked our wounds and tried to begin anew, I reflected on how I had violated almost every rule for using self-disclosure appropriately. I ignored what she needed in order to do what I needed at the time. I misinterpreted the cues as to how she was reacting to my disclosure and blundered on obliviously. I had become more forceful than was called for. And I took the lazy way out by using an intervention that was convenient for me rather than appropriate for her.

Of course, with hindsight, it is always easier to analyze what we should have tried or should not have done. The fact is that *because* self-disclosure can have such a powerful effect, it is best used cautiously, in moderation, and only when we are certain that it is in the client's best interests.

Dealing with Endings

I remember that in all the texts I used as a graduate student, the books I read subsequently, the workshops I attended, and the supervision I received, I was told repeatedly about the importance of *termination*. Although that very word struck terror in my mind (conjuring up images of turning off someone's life support system), I came to appreciate the importance of ending the therapy relationship on a productive note so that the previous work would not be undone. I always felt that this was, among all the other therapeutic tasks, the most difficult—not only for the client but for me. When clients leave treatment, I sometimes feel abandoned, sometimes elated and relieved, sometimes sad, but always I feel *something*. Clients, of course, also carry around a lot of unexpressed as well as overt feelings about us, about the therapy, and about things coming to a close.

I learned that termination is something that should be prepared for weeks and sometimes months in advance. I was taught that clients should give plenty of notice before they stop treatment so there is enough time to work through all their unresolved issues (yes, like most graduate students, I thought it was possible, someday, to be finished, once and for all, with one's issues). I was exposed to a series of steps one should go through when ending therapy, much like a pilot preparing for a landing. These included things like: mutually agree that the time is appropriate to draw things to a close, slowly wind down the frequency and intensity of sessions, summarize the work that has been done, identify areas the client may wish to continue to work on independently, offer support and encouragement, work through resistances and ambivalence to ending, and schedule a follow-up visit sometime in the future.

You can therefore imagine my surprise when I discovered that in the real world of daily practice this neat progression hardly ever occurred. Most often clients would end therapy by simply canceling an appointment and never again rescheduling another. Sometimes they might do this because of trouble with intimacy or letting go; other times, therapy ends this way because it is expedient for both partners who want to say goodbye but feel awkward about it.

Effective therapists are skilled at trying to help their clients end in a way, *any* way, that allows them to feel good about their work and continue to be their own therapist in the future (Kupers, 1988; Kramer, 1990). Indeed, the transition from being in therapy to not being in therapy is a difficult transition to manage — for both participants. It is likely that some dependence has developed. The client has come to look forward to the regular talks, the intimacy, the accountability to a concerned and wise mentor who gives such wonderful input. The client remembers all too well what things were like before treatment began, and although the client is now quite a different person, he or she cannot help but wonder whether, once the sessions cease, the old problems will recur.

For many weeks, months, perhaps years, the client has participated in a structure that has produced wondrous results. What will happen when it stops? Will he or she be able to continue growth without benefit of the expert's help?

The answers to these questions depend, to a great extent, on the therapist's skill in ending the therapeutic encounter. And there are several distinct skills involved.

Recognizing That the Time Is Right. If done appropriately, this is most often a mutual decision, especially when the client has been helped all along to assess where he or she is in relation to desired goals. Sometimes the cues signaling that the client is ready to go it alone are more subtle: (1) evidence of disengagement or slowed pace in sessions, (2) a number of missed or canceled appointments, (3) difficulty finding new areas to work on, and (4) a lack of compliance with therapeutic tasks.

The hard part is determining when resistance is a sign that there is a lot more work to do once blocks are removed, versus a signal that it is time for things to end. I have always thought it interesting that this decision is so often influenced by the setting in which therapy is practiced. In agencies where there is a waiting list of prospective clients, hesitation, reluctance, and slowed pace are more often interpreted as signals that the client is ready to end sessions, whereas in private practice where the clinician's livelihood depends on the ability to hold onto clients, quite a different interpretation may be made. Whatever criteria are used, or whatever the setting in which therapy is practiced, there are opportune times to begin closing.

Preparing the Client for Ending Therapy. Transitions are always difficult, and especially so if they have not been anticipated. Effective therapists continue to reinforce these messages to their clients: "I appreciate your gratitude, but *you* are the one who has done most of the work. *You* are the one who has worked so hard on yourself, who has taken such risks, who has changed the way you think and feel and behave so dramatically. And because *you* have done these things here, you can continue this growth on your own."

The client is helped to realize that:

- Therapy is not magic; it is the result of a systematically applied way of thinking and problem solving that has already been internalized.

- It is indeed an appropriate time to move on. Evidence is reviewed of all the progress that has been made, what was done, and how it was done.
- When inevitable setbacks occur, there are many things the client knows how to do that have proven useful previously.
- Although the therapist may no longer be physically present in the client's life, the therapist will always be a part of him or her in spirit. The therapist's voice has become the client's voice, at least in part.

Structuring a Gradual Transition. The trauma of ending therapy can be minimized when the client is gradually weaned of dependency issues and the need for regular checkups. Not all clients require such deliberate programs; some simply announce one week they feel ready to try things on their own for a while. Other clients need weeks, perhaps months of discussion and practice in order to work toward ending.

The universal skill in all therapies is helping clients to maintain their continued growth once the sessions have ended. This is accomplished by working through unfinished business and parting on the best of terms. It also involves providing a structure and support after things have ended, as well as leaving the door open for follow-up work as needed. Some people believe that therapy never ceases, that clients continue their dialogues with us (as they do with deceased parents) for the rest of their lives.

In Summary

"Compleat" therapists have much in common in terms of their technical proficiency. Apart from any specific philosophies and theoretical positions they may hold, good clinicians have mastered a set of universal, core skills. These are adapted to the unique personality and situation of each practitioner. They are easily recognizable in the behavior of most effective therapists, who can readily demonstrate their ability to be empathic or confrontational or insightful, depending on what is required.

Being an effective therapist involves much more than applying a set of technical skills and interventions when they are called for. There is a distinctly passionate, human quality to the performance of a virtuoso in any field. We do not use skills as a plumber or electrician would employ tools; rather, through training, practice, and dedication, we have made therapeutic skills part of our very being — like breathing. The most accomplished therapists do not just *act* like compassionate and skilled helpers; they *are* effective precisely because they do not have to act.

CHAPTER SEVEN

How the Joys and Challenges
of Therapeutic Work
Translate into Effective Therapy

Jarmel is a woman I have worked with for many years. The first year of our relationship — when she was sixteen — was among the most difficult I have ever lived through as a therapist. She was so depressed that much of the time I could hardly stand to be in the same room with her. She would cry constantly — great wracking sobs that would punctuate a steady stream of tears and hopelessness: "I've always been this way and I probably always will be. There's nothing you or I or anyone else can do about it."

And this was not the worst of it.

While being with someone who is so obviously and chronically miserable is certainly trying, it is even harder for me to tolerate manipulative mind games. Whatever Jarmel lacked in a zest for life, she more than made up for in her skills at remaining inscrutable and obstinate. There were whole sessions that would go by in which she would not say a word. She would just hide behind her hair, and alternately cry or smile at my feeble attempts to engage her. She seemed to be laughing at me, at my sense of powerlessness and ineptitude. And still she would remain desperately depressed.

Jarmel seemed to delight in my discomfort. I sometimes thought that was the only reason she returned — to torment me by reminding me of my own inability to connect with her. Weeks

175

turned into months. I called her parents to try to end the sessions. I explained that I did not feel that we were making much progress. Yet her parents were so preoccupied with their own busy lives that they were relieved to have someone else available to be with her. So I was a kidsitter. And if I could help Jarmel, I was of some use in relieving her parents' guilt.

Jarmel and I both felt stuck with one another; there could be no escape for either one of us. Eventually, she seemed to grow bored with her passive, helpless, tearful role — or perhaps she began to feel sorry for me. In any case, she would now come in and chatter on demand. She would talk about school, drugs, boys, friends, offering nonstop monologues that were at once frantic and amusing. It was as if this filibuster about the events in her daily life would occupy our time, but in such a way that I could not make contact with her. I felt like I was not even in the same room.

When Jarmel left for college at age eighteen, I felt as if I had been granted a parole. Here was this girl who I had spent hundreds of hours with, yet I hardly knew her. I hated her. And I loved her. I have never worked so hard to know somebody, and I have never felt more rebuffed. I had tried everything I knew how to do and did not make a dent.

I must admit that I felt more than a little relieved when, over the next few years, I received several phone calls from a succession of new therapists who were working with Jarmel. Psychiatrists, psychologists, neurologists, social workers — she slew them all. Every few months I would get another frustrated and confused letter or call from a professional wanting input in the case. One day, a call came from Jarmel herself, wanting to schedule a session.

It had been two years since our last meeting. I felt nervous, apprehensive, curious, excited, all at once. What would she be like? Would she be cooperative? Could I do anything for her now?

To my surprise, she was both calm and cordial. We caught up on her life and what had transpired during the intervening years. As I looked at her and noticed how different she appeared, I reflected on how I had changed as well since the last time we met. I had rearranged the furniture in my office. And I am certain my style of practice had evolved as well.

We began working together again, but this time it felt different for both of us. There was a closeness, a genuine caring I felt from her, and I know she could feel the same from me. She was spontaneous, articulate, perceptive, and hardworking. Sometimes she became depressed, but the feelings did not last long.

On one occasion, she was able to trace the beginnings of her depression. She recalled not only the times she had felt immobilized and despondent, but how each of her family members reacted to her. Her father's response had the greatest impact. When she became depressed, he would initially try to confront her, but he would eventually grow frustrated, angry, and then rejecting. All she had wanted was for her father to understand, but he had been too frightened, too impatient, and too frustrated (it certainly sounded familiar to me in our relationship).

We decided to invite Jarmel's father in for a joint session to try to resolve some of these issues. They both appeared somewhat shy and tentative in each other's presence. Jarmel looked at me with a pleading expression that seemed to be saying, "Are you sure this is necessary?" I nodded reassuringly.

On cue, Jarmel unloaded all the pent-up feelings of rejection, fear, and anger she had toward her father. Why couldn't he have comforted her more? Why was he so afraid of her moods? Why couldn't he share more of himself with her?

Haltingly, he explained what it was like for him to see her in pain. He *had* tried to reach out to her, but in turn, had felt closed out. He stopped trying to comfort her only because he thought she wanted to be left alone.

I was watching this interchange open-mouthed and astonished. I felt so privileged to be part of this deeply emotional moment between father and daughter. Yet I did not feel like I was intruding; I had earned the right to be there by the dues I had paid over the years—staying in there with Jarmel when we both wanted nothing else but to be rid of one another.

At one magical moment, Jarmel and her father embraced tentatively, then began a fierce hug. They both started crying. And then I was crying too.

As father and daughter walked out of the office, arms around each other, I was left alone with the residue of what had happened. I felt thoroughly drained, and I could not recall another time that I had experienced such elation. My gosh, what an incredible honor to do this work that can sometimes lead to earth-shaking, life-changing experiences! Through the drudgery, the battles and boredom and pressure, through the blistering intensity, there sometimes emerges a single event or act or moment that rewards all the hard work and time we have invested.

The challenge of being a therapist is sharing the joy of others during their moments of discovery and redemption. It is at such times that we are blessed with a form of spiritual transcendence, of perfect love, and of a heightened existence that has no boundaries.

Freedom in Being a Therapist

What helps to make therapists most effective and influential is their enthusiasm. In any activity or line of work, the more we like doing something, the more energy we will devote to trying to do it well. Therapists who enjoy their work, who feel excited about what they are doing, who anticipate their sessions with relish, are going to be more successful than their peers who are simply going through the motions.

Experience and years of service seem to have a way of tempering one's enthusiasm. Novelty gives way to the routine. Yet many veteran practitioners have been able to retain the enchantment of their work, and in so doing, increase their satisfaction and effectiveness.

Many of the satisfactions that are part of a therapist's life have been described in various sources (Farber and Heifetz, 1981; Marston, 1984; Kottler, 1986; Guy, 1987). Therapists who enjoy their work most tend to be those who have a great deal of independence, flexible hours, a relaxed work setting, and a sense of accomplishment that is recognized by others (Tryon, 1983; Farber, 1985a).

To do this kind of work requires a certain amount of freedom: freedom in the way we work, in the way we structure our practice, in the variety of activities that we can participate in. A day in the life of a typical therapist can include client sessions that are trying, frustrating, stimulating, confusing, tearful, joyful, stressful, and boring. And interspaced between these encounters (hopefully) are periods for rest and reflection. There are opportunities for discussing cases with peers. There is time for catching up on reading and paperwork. There are meetings to attend, calls to return, and people to touch base with.

There is also freedom with respect to whom we work with. Some clinicians have developed a specialty that they prefer to exercise whenever possible. Others have the freedom to see a variety of cases or work in a variety of modalities: groups, marital or conjoint sessions, family or individual sessions. Joy in being a therapist seems to come most often from the freedom to facilitate our own personal growth as a corollary of our professional endeavors.

Personal Growth of Therapists

Many believe that the greatest benefit that occurs to those who practice psychotherapy is their own continued personal growth (Farber, 1983; Goldberg, 1986; Guy, 1987). Jung (1961, p. 145) remarked in a retrospective on his professional life that "from my encounters with patients and with the psychic phenomena which they have paraded before me in an endless stream of images, I have learned an enormous amount — not just knowledge, but above all, insight into my own nature." The act of facilitating change in others can inspire, in ourselves, a similar growth process in which we are forced to confront our unresolved issues. As we help clients to explore the major themes of life — meaning and purpose, priorities, aspirations, relationships, fears, and death — we conduct an internal dialogue about these very subjects and our own responses to them.

I have noticed that three different times today alone my buttons were pushed by interactions with clients. An adolescent talks about how important it is for him to be with his friends. So what, he says, if his grades are not that good, or he is not so productive — he feels very nurtured and cared for by his close friends.

And I think to myself: Oops. Am I jealous! I want to say: Right kid! You *do* have things straight! But of course I do not. I do, however, resolve to make developing relationships more of a priority.

Next client walks in. A woman about my age. She discloses she is thinking of having another baby, but wonders if she might be too old. Before I respond to her, I ponder my own feelings on this issue and am startled to discover that although I had finally decided *that* stage in my life was over, I begin to wonder . . .

The third client of the day brings in an old standby sure to elicit terror in me every time I hear it mentioned. As she begins talking about her fear of losing control and doing something really stupid or destructive, I begin to drift into my own stuff again.

I know there is that old joke about the younger therapist asking the veteran how he sits and listens to his clients day after day and yet always appears so unruffled and tranquil. He of course replies, "Easy. I don't listen." How can we listen to our clients and avoid being touched deeply by what we hear? And I do not mean moved only by compassion and empathy, but shaken at our core by the incredibly meaningful and intense subject we discuss every day.

One would hope we would get pretty good at dealing with our own conflicts after spending so much time working with those of others. If professional carpenters can build themselves nice living spaces in their free time, it only makes sense that therapists would apply what they know to themselves as well. After years of experience, we become more confident in our ability to converse intelligently, to understand the complexities of human behavior, and to read a situation and know what will work. We thus become attuned to ourselves as we develop a sensitivity to others. We get quite good at figuring out what we are personally experiencing and then articulating clearly these thoughts and feelings.

Many unresolved personal issues affect our work. While these countertransference conflicts do not exactly fit under the category of "joys of being a therapist," the necessity of resolving them in order to operate effectively is indeed a tremendous benefit of our profession.

Kroll (1988, pp. 186–187) has constructed a schematic model to summarize the therapist's countertransference issues as they are played out in sessions: "The therapy situation is the arena in which the therapist works out her own issues during the process of working with the patient. These issues are always present, to differing degrees, in all therapists, since we are humans first and therapists second."

Kroll organizes the therapist's personal issues according to those in which he or she becomes self-protective versus the opposite polarity of being exploitative. In the former modality, actions are taken to protect oneself against vulnerability and certain core issues: the fear of criticism, the fear of engulfment, the fear of being seduced, the fear of passivity, and the fear of being correct. These same countertransference themes are also manifested in the ways that therapists attempt to meet their own needs through exploitation: the need to be flattered, the need to be a caretaker, the need to be sexually desirable, the need to be in control, and the need to be correct.

Whereas everyone struggles with these personal issues, what distinguishes the effective clinician is the degree to which he or she has acknowledged and worked through them. While not immune to flattery or to the pleasure that comes from being correct, being liked and appreciated, or being in control, effective therapists guard against acting out their own issues during sessions.

Mutual Impact

It is the scourge of our work that it is difficult to hide from our own issues when we are constantly being assailed by the fears and anxieties of others. But it is also our greatest privilege.

Whether we like it or not, we feel an irresistible urge to keep growing and changing in our lives as we witness the changes in others. We are like travel agents who book trips all day long to wonderful and exotic places. Our clients return with tales of their adventures, of places they visited, and of experiences they have had.

After so many hours, days, and weeks of listening to people make changes in their lives, it is hard for us not to want to join them. I feel envious of the opportunities clients have created for themselves. While I sit in my insulated office with a window to the outside world, listening to the stories people bring of the new things they have done, I sometimes feel left behind.

I hear a client tell of risks she has taken to initiate new social contacts, and it spurs me on to do the same. Another reports making a mid-life career change for the sake of greater stimulation and challenge, and I feel a sympathetic tug to do something similar. Someone else proclaims he is sick of his endless search for power and wealth and thereby plots a new direction for his life; it strikes a chord within me as well. I hear someone else decide she had overworked and overscheduled herself and it is time to make some changes. She takes a three-month leave of absence and travels around the world. I think to myself, I could do that too. What is stopping me?

With each of these clients, or for that matter, with every client we see, there is a mutual exchange of ideas, values, and influence. It is truly one of the greatest joys of our profession that, just as a travel agent gets reduced rates for personal trips, we have special incentives to stay committed to our own personal growth. On a daily basis, we are confronted with our most poignant issues and thus spurred on to do something about resolving them. This process is described by one clinician in the context of explaining how he believes changes occur in therapy:

> Mary was a client of mine who brought into the therapeutic process the heaviness of an overburdened life, a life of constant service that exhausted her and left virtually no space or time for silence, for letting things unfold gradually, and for her own leisure and responsiveness to inner time. Her life was ruled by the clock. Everything was timed and her activities had to be accomplished hurriedly.
>
> As she described the constant demands on her life and the absence of space to stretch freely, it was clear to me that while I listened with concern and caring, she was also listening to herself and realizing that only she could choose to change the pat-

tern, only she could halt the destructiveness of exhaustion and of overburdening herself. My supportive presence, regard for her, and the hope and promise I sensed in her exploration facilitated her resolution to change. Together we developed a course of action in which she would begin a process of terminating several activities, freeing herself for other alternatives that would be edifying and self-enhancing.

I was also surprised to realize that I, too, share Mary's problem and resolved to make a similar change in cutting down the activities in my life. The act of writing this down feels good in that I am committing myself to follow through on what I want to do.

The Challenges of Practice

Psychotherapy is very much like a serialized drama in which each week new episodes are produced. However, for the therapist, there is an interactive role that permits active participation in the production. We are neither part of the audience that watches passively as the story unfolds nor are we the central protagonist who suffers the pain and anguish of the journey. We stand backstage, close to the action but able to intervene from a distance if redirection is indicated. And what excitement is in store for us as we eagerly await the next installment from our clients!

In a volume of essays on what lead prominent therapists into the profession, Bloomfield (1989, p. 47) described what is, for her, the essence of her mission: "The most common feeling I have when I think about being a therapist is one of awe. Perhaps it is a little of the way parents might feel when they observe the unfolding of their young child's personality. This probably sounds rather grandiose, but the feeling has to be acknowledged. I appreciate it particularly, though, when a patient begins to find his or her autonomy, and gaining my approval or disapproval is no longer a priority."

Practicing therapy effectively is the ultimate rush of exhilaration. There is intimacy. There is intensity. There is unpredictability and spontaneity. There is complete honesty and vulnerability. There is the self, unadorned and naked. There is compassion. And finally, there is opportunity without limits — the chance to change anything and everything within one's domain.

In an initial encounter with a client, there is nervous anticipation and excitement. A new challenge. A new test of our resources and powers to be inventive and creative. We are offered a new life to study, a new person we will come to know. We are presented with a puzzle to put together, one that has stumped many others before us. We are invited to witness the client's life story, to be privy to his or her deepest, darkest secrets. And with each journey we take to the furthest reaches of human experience, we return, as from any trip, wiser and renewed.

Being Useful

Yalom (1980) has stated that being useful to others is among the most powerful sources of meaning in life. Who can describe what it feels like when a client looks at us with such gratitude, such admiration and love, says goodbye, and then confidently walks out the door? We remember this same person at first meeting — hesitant, timid, inarticulate, confused, tense, and uncomfortable. And then we think back on all that has transpired since that time, unable to quite remember how and when things changed.

We draw comfort from these occasional but regular transformations in which we *know* we made a difference in the world, playing our small part in reducing needless suffering. There are other times when we seriously wonder whether anything we do really matters.

Dass and Gorman (1985, p. 50) talk about the importance of the questions: What have we really accomplished in our lives? How have we been useful? What does everything we have done really mean? "It could mean that when we're holding a frightened, battered child . . . or hearing the grief of a total stranger . . . or bandaging the wound of an enemy soldier . . . or sitting with a dying friend . . . they can feel in *who we are* the reassurance that they are not simply isolated entities, separate selves, lonely beings, cut off from everything and everyone else. They can feel us *in there* with them. They can feel the comfort that we are all of us in this together. They have the chance to know, in moments of great pain, that nevertheless we are Not Separate."

This brings us to the subject of altruism. Two recent studies on altruism found that people who help others actually experience a release of endorphins similar to a "runner's high" that results in increased energy, a sense of well-being, and inner calmness. Furthermore, these sensations of strength and pleasure can be accessed every time the helper relives the events (Luks, 1988). This would be consistent with what we know about the evolution of the nervous system, which has been designed to reward those behaviors likely to increase the survival of one's collective gene pool. What is perplexing to sociobiologists is how to reconcile the drive to maximize one's own offspring versus those demands to protect the welfare of others. In other words, without some reciprocal payoff for the risks and energy involved, any effort expended to help someone else is likely to be detrimental to one's own chances of survival and those of family members. Yet, time and time again, people and animals will risk their lives and welfare to help others. Birds will give warning calls at the appearance of a hawk and thereby sacrifice themselves to save the flock. Dolphins and elephants will help other wounded animals of their kind rather than leaving them to die. Gazelles, baboons, and other animals will also jeopardize their safety to protect the group (Singer, 1981).

This suggests that performing unselfish acts is intrinsically satisfying. But let us be open about this. People are not only in this profession because they like it; some are in it for the money. It is not that these two things cannot go together — that we should not be well compensated for our expertise — but that those who are motivated *primarily* by monetary rather than altruistic rewards will measure their satisfaction in terms of fees collected instead of people who are helped. That we are paid for what we do, and often paid well, is an unexpected bonus in a life devoted to serving others.

Those of us who have been practicing a while often forget what led us to this work initially — not dreams of fame and fortune, but images of people who are now smiling rather than crying because of time we spent with them. Once we lose sight of our altruism and dedication to the cause of emotional health, we become immersed in our own hapless search for recognition, material comforts, and power and control in relationships. We become automatons, getting the clients in and out and thinking in terms of billable hours, marketing strategies, productivity, efficiency.

One therapist I interviewed, who is presumably not alone in his choice of life-style, shares a disturbing picture: "I see between forty-five and fifty clients per week, every week. I also have a group I run and some administrative things I take care of. I've been doing this for years, so long I don't even think about it any longer. Sometimes I might see seven, eight, nine people back to back without a break. I just sort of get in a groove, almost like an assembly line. Why do I do this, you ask? Because I've got bills to pay."

When the joy is gone, what is left is a job like any other. It is a matter of putting in time, getting through the day, making money, spending money. And what is lost is the almost magical appreciation for the stories that are told, the lives that we touch, the mysteries that we are able to see and help unravel. Bach (1966, p. 5) describes the joy that we often experience on the therapeutic journey we take part in: "To see the unseen! To see light where apparently there is only darkness, hope where there is seemingly nothing but despair, faith when it is crowded out by fear, the hint of joy when it appears there can never be anything but sorrow, victory in the shattering hour of defeat, and love when all seems engulfed by hate! Give me that vision, for that which I see is that which unalterably comes to pass."

The Essence of Effective Psychotherapy

We have examined the essence of effective therapy along several dimensions — the qualities of exemplary practitioners, the characteristic ways in which they think, and the skills and interventions they have mastered. And indeed, as Jaspers (1963) points out, the process of therapeutic change is so complex that we are likely never to understand fully what happens and why, nor will we ever reduce its essence to a few skills, concepts, or variables.

In trying to explain effective therapy, Watzlawick (1986, p. 93) has offered an interesting perspective: "If that little green man from Mars arrived and asked us to explain our techniques for affecting human change, and if we then told him, would he not scratch his head (or its equivalent) in disbelief and ask us why we have arrived at such complicated, abstruse and far-fetched theories, rather than first of all investigating how human change comes about naturally, spontaneously, and on an everyday basis?"

People change when they are ready to assume responsibility for their lives, their choices, their behavior. They quite simply decide to be different. "To decide means to commit oneself to an action and to carry it out. . . . Some patients say, 'yes, I know what is to be done now. Thank you for helping me see the alternatives more clearly. I want to straighten out this mess, quit hurting myself and other people. I'll do it.' They say goodbye and, in follow-up, report that change has gone according to plan. Neat and clean" (Beitman, 1987, p. 188).

More often, however, Beitman believes this decision to take charge of one's life is made unconsciously, in a series of small, incremental steps. "They cross the narrow footbridge of change in pieces, like an amoeba slowly bringing parts of itself into new territory, yet able to withdraw committed parts at a moment's notice" (p. 188).

I have been working with Melanie for some time. As I look at her, it is hard for me to remember that she was ever different than she is now. Suffering from a debilitating chronic illness, her life is a continual struggle to manage the symptoms of her disease and the side effects of her medications. She is uncomfortable much of the time and complains a lot. She feels sorry for herself. Her depression is voracious.

Even before the first physical symptoms struck, she was tough to deal with: negative, complaining, fearful, harried by her children, discouraged by a life that felt empty. There was never a single juncture in which Melanie decided to stop whining and complaining, stop blaming others for her plight, and just get get on with the business of living. At first she made a few feeble efforts to stop complaining about how much she hates to be a mother. While she still felt overwhelmed by the demands of four children under the age of ten, she decided to stop wishing that things could be different.

Somewhere along the line, she made a number of other decisions regarding her self-responsibility: (1) that her life did not have to be boring and empty — she got a job to give herself time away from the house and to enrich her days; (2) that she need not feel guilty for "abandoning" her family a few days a week — she confronted her mother's attempts at guilt inducement; (3) that she need not accept mediocrity in the intimacy levels with her husband and friends — she tried being more open regarding her needs; (4) that although she could not change the status of her physical health, she could choose the way she thinks and feels about it and the way she lives the time available to her.

My role in all of this is similar, I believe, to what most therapists would do. I helped her to let go of things she could not do anything about and focus her energy on areas that were within her power to control, most notably her attitudes and perceptions about self and the world. At various times I used the methodologies of practically every approach I am familiar with, and while their routes and mechanisms may appear different, the ultimate goal for her and for me was the same — to help her decide to change. This was accomplished through compassionate listening at some points and vigorous confrontations or integrative interpretations at others. Whatever I did, or however I worked, seemed to lead us in the same direction anyway.

As I look over the stack of progress notes from the past years, I can see no single point in which Melanie ever decided to give up her complaining, externalizing, and depression. It happened gradually, imperceptibly, and usually with great reluctance. Her last decisions have yet to be made — to live the rest of her days with a feeling of personal power and to die with dignity. But in time, I am confident she will accept responsibility for those choices as well. Maybe it is *that* belief — the faith and optimism that members of our profession universally share — that truly makes it possible for clients such as Melanie to make new choices about the ways they wish to be.

We can make the task of understanding how people change, and how effective therapists operate, so very complicated. At its most rudimentary level, the process of therapy is one in which an environment is created that is especially fertile for growth. Lots of nutrients. Near-perfect weather conditions. Pruning when needed. But basically clients change when they feel ready to. The effective therapist waits patiently, and keeps trying different things to help the client feel ready to change. Some of these things are done to entertain the client, some to educate, and some to offer structure or disrupt existing patterns. Eventually, one of these things clicks.

We have seen how, regardless of professional specialty, orientation, or theoretical assumptions, psychotherapy follows a similar path for most people. While this interaction is far too complex to allow us to discern all the subtle factors that contribute to the interaction and consequent changes, psychological influence is produced by any and all of the following:

1. The force and power of the therapist's personality
2. A therapeutic relationship that is permissive, intimate, and trusting
3. The application of interventions designed to:
   - Motivate the client to take risks
   - Facilitate self-understanding
   - Reinforce desirable qualities
   - Eliminate dysfunctional behaviors
   - Initiate new patterns
   - Improve confidence and self-esteem
   - Offer support and encouragement

The compleat therapist is the embodiment of all that makes a compleat human being — compassion, competence, confidence, wisdom. In addition, he or she is a superb communicator and is exquisitely sensitive to the inner world of others. It matters little what professional specialty he or she is trained in, or which theoretical approach that specialty rests on. What matters most is a clarity of mind, a tranquillity of spirit, and a disciplined set of interventions that may be relied on as needed. And more than all of these things, the effective therapist is a kind and caring human being who knows how to love others without exploiting them, who knows how to nurture without fostering dependency, and who can teach others to teach themselves.

Working Toward Greater Effectiveness

Throughout this book we have explored a number of therapeutic variables, personal attributes, thinking processes, and process skills that, when combined in unique ways, make up the essence of a compleat therapist. This is naturally an ideal model of functioning—one that we are all striving toward greater mastery of.

As a way of summarizing the themes covered in this book, it may be helpful to review the factors previously discussed in a way that will facilitate a self-assessment process. Specifically, it may be constructive to examine your own functioning according to the degree of mastery you have attained in each of following dimensions. This scale asks you to rate each item on a continuum as to how descriptive it is of you, from "Very Descriptive" to "Very Unlike" the way you work. You may delete items that are not relevant to your style of practice or not part of what you consider to be important ("Not Relevant").

Unlike those little quizzes in *Reader's Digest* or other magazines, there is no score to calculate that tells you how you compare to your peers. Rather, the objective of this self-assessment exercise is to highlight those aspects of your functioning that may help you to become even more effective as a therapist. Consider each item on this list. Which of the following responses do you have to each statement?

- Very descriptive of me
- Somewhat descriptive of me
- Unsure if this describes me

- Somewhat unlike me
- Very unlike me
- Not relevant to the way in which I work

Capitalizing on Therapeutic Variables

I encourage an open sharing of feeling and thoughts.

I maintain the client's interest, motivation, and commitment.

I establish a productive therapeutic alliance.

I influence perceptions and alter awarenesses.

I encourage clients to explore the unknown.

I promote self-acceptance.

I foster positive expectations.

I encourage independence and autonomy.

I provide opportunities for practicing new ways of thinking and acting.

I facilitate the completion of tasks designed to reach client goals.

Personal Attributes

I am deeply and passionately committed to my work.

I model the qualities of a powerful, dynamic, vibrant person.

I am confident in my ability to be helpful.

I accept clients unconditionally, even if I selectively accept certain behaviors over others.

I appear serene, relaxed, and at ease.

I have high functional intelligence and "street smarts" that permit me to understand people and their worlds.

I inspire trust.

I appear authentic and congruent.

I exude warmth and caring for others.

I communicate respect for clients as important people.

I am willing to admit my mistakes and misjudgments.

I am persuasive in encouraging clients to take risks.

I am self-accepting and comfortable in my body and mind.

I present myself as an attractive human being who others would wish to emulate.

I exercise self-restraint in not meeting my own needs in sessions.

I am willing to acknowledge, confront, and work through my unresolved personal issues.

I am willing to solicit help or consultations when I feel stuck.

Internal Processing

I am adaptable and flexible in my thinking.

I have a high tolerance for ambiguity, abstraction, and complexity.

I have developed an efficient system of information storage and retrieval.

I can establish connections between seemingly unrelated behaviors.

I am able to make inferences regarding future or past behaviors based on present functioning.

I am familiar with a range of disciplines and have a vast pool of knowledge from which to draw metaphors.

I am sensitive to nuances in behavior as well as underlying or unexpressed feelings.

I can recognize patterns amidst confusing, jumbled data.

I employ flexible cognitive schemata that permit further growth and evolution.

I am incisive and accurate in my perceptions of "reality."

I have sound clinical judgment regarding case management.

I am able to reduce complex phenomena to their essences.

I am able to discover multiple cause-effect relationships of the same phenomenon.

I recognize those critical moments when an intervention is needed.

Process Skills

I demonstrate high levels of empathic resonance.

I am able to confront and challenge nondefensively.

I can identify and reflect feelings.

I summarize client experiences concisely and accurately.

I reinforce fully functioning behaviors while extinguishing those that are self-defeating.

I use self-disclosure powerfully yet sparingly.

I use role induction methods to teach clients how to get
the most from therapy.

I offer high levels of support and reassurance.

I correct distortions of reality evident in client statements
or behaviors.

I interpret accurately and fully the underlying meanings
of behavior.

I set limits and boundaries regarding appropriate conduct in therapy.

I am technically proficient in applying the core skills of
communication and helping.

Reviewing this list is an intimidating experience—even more
so when we realize that this is only a small sampling of those
factors that go into making a therapist effective. Nevertheless,
this self-assessment helps us to identify patterns in our functioning that point to the ways we operate most and least effectively.
Finally, this review also reminds us to beware of those who think
they have discovered *the* correct way to do therapy—not only
for themselves, but for everyone else.

In Summary

You have probably read this book for the same reasons I wrote
it. We are all interested in a better understanding of what a compleat therapist is. Most of us want to know how we are doing,
especially compared to our peers. Our clients seem to be improving, but what if it is an illusion? What if they are not improving as much as they could if they were working with someone else—someone who knows more than we do, someone who
can be or do more than we can? We all know professionals who
seem brighter than we are, wiser, more skilled, better trained,
yes, more effective. The question immediately comes to mind,
What are they offering that I am not? We assume that with more
study, more experience, more dedication, we too can be as effective as they are—or at least can reach our own potential. Yet
if there is one thing I have learned from this intensive survey

of what characterizes the most effective therapists, it is that there is no specific thing they know or do. Rather, it is a certain feeling inside them.

I started this book with the perplexing question of how it is possible that effective therapists can be so varied. They are nurturing or confrontational, they can work in the past or the present, or they operate in the domain of feelings, thoughts, or behaviors. They can be stern or playful in their interactions. They can be trained as psychiatrists, nurses, social workers, counselors, or psychologists. They can talk a lot or a little. They can be formal or informal, structured or loose in the process they offer. So what, then, allows so many different personalities, styles, and therapeutic approaches to be effective? What makes *you* most helpful to others?

I believe the answer is found in the essence of who we are as human beings. If we can be clear about and unencumbered by our own personal issues, if we can be fully present with the client, if we can exude a certain amount of warmth and wisdom, if we believe that what we are doing (whatever that is) is going to be helpful, then we are more likely to be effective as influencers and facilitators of growth. Add to this an expertise in some specialty, and what we have is a compleat therapist who most often makes a difference by believing in himself or herself.

References

Alexander, F., and French, T. M. *Psychoanalytic Therapy: Principles and Applications.* New York: Ronald Press, 1946.

Arkes, H. R. "Impediments to Accurate Clinical Judgment and Possible Ways to Minimize Their Input." *Journal of Consulting and Clinical Psychology,* 1981, *49,* 323–330.

Arnkoff, D. B. "Common and Specific Factors in Cognitive Therapy." In M. J. Lambert (ed.), *Psychotherapy and Patient Relationships.* Homewood, Ill.: Dorsey Press, 1983.

Arnoult, L. H., and Anderson, C. A. "Identifying and Reducing Causal Reasoning Biases in Clinical Practice." In D. C. Turk and P. Salovey (eds.), *Reasoning, Inference, and Judgment in Clinical Psychology.* New York: Free Press, 1988.

Bach, M. *The Power of Perception.* New York: Doubleday, 1966.

Bandler, R., and Grinder, J. *The Structure of Magic.* Palo Alto, Calif.: Science and Behavior Books, 1975.

Bandura, A. *Principles of Behavior Modification.* New York: Holt, Rinehart & Winston, 1969.

Bandura, A. "Self-Efficacy: Toward a Unifying Theory of Behavioral Change." *Psychological Review,* 1977, *84,* 191–215.

Barnard, G. W., Fuller, K., Robbins, L., and Shaw, T. *The Child Molester: An Integrated Approach to Evaluation and Treatment.* New York: Brunner/Mazel, 1989.

Basch, M. *Understanding Psychotherapy.* New York: Basic Books, 1988.

Beitman, B. D. *The Structure of Individual Psychotherapy.* New York: Guilford Press, 1987.

Beitman, B. D., Goldfried, M. R., and Norcross, J. C. "The Movement Toward Integrating the Psychotherapies: An Overview." *American Journal of Psychiatry,* 1989, *146* (2), 138–147.

Benderly, B. L. "Intuition Every Day." *Psychology Today,* Sept. 1989, pp. 35–40.

Bergman, J. S. *Fishing for Barracuda.* New York: Norton, 1985.

Bernstein, A. "The Psychoanalytic Technique." In B. B. Wolman (ed.), *Handbook of Clinical Psychology.* New York: McGraw-Hill, 1965.

Beutler, L. E. *Eclectic Psychotherapy: A Systematic Approach.* New York: Pergamon Press, 1983.

Beutler, L. E. "Systematic Eclectic Psychotherapy." In J. C. Norcross (ed.), *Handbook of Eclectic Psychotherapy.* New York: Brunner/Mazel, 1986.

Beutler, L. E., Crago, M., and Arizmendi, T. G. "Therapist Variables in Psychotherapy Process and Outcome." In S. L. Garfield and A. E. Bergin (eds.), *Handbook of Psychotherapy and Behavior Change.* (3rd ed.) New York: Wiley, 1986.

Birk, L., and Brinkley-Birk, A. W. "Psychoanalysis and Behavior Therapy." *American Journal of Psychiatry,* 1974, *131,* 499–510.

Bloomfield, I. "Through Therapy to Self." In W. Dryden and L. Spurling (eds.), *On Becoming a Psychotherapist.* London: Tavistock/Routledge, 1989.

Bongar, B., Peterson, L. G., Harris, E. A., and Aissis, J. "Clinical and Legal Considerations in the Management of Suicidal Patients: An Integrative Overview." *Journal of Integrative and Eclectic Psychotherapy,* 1989, *8,* 264–276.

Boorstin, D. *The Discoverers.* New York: Random House, 1983.

Brammer, L. M., and Shostrum, E. L. *Therapeutic Psychology.* (4th ed.) Englewood Cliffs, N.J.: Prentice-Hall, 1982.

Brehm, S. S., and Smith, T. W. "Social Psychological Approaches to Psychotherapy and Behavior Change." In S. L. Garfield and A. E. Bergin (eds.), *Handbook of Psychotherapy and Behavior Change.* (3rd ed.) New York: Wiley, 1986.

Brunick, S., and Schroeder, H. "Verbal Therapeutic Behavior

of Expert Psychoanalytically Oriented, Gestalt, and Behavior Therapists." *Journal of Consulting and Clinical Psychology,* 1979, *47,* 567–574.

Budman, S. H., and Gurman, A. S. *Theory and Practice of Brief Therapy.* New York: Guilford Press, 1988.

Bugental, J. F. T. *Psychotherapy and Process.* Reading, Mass.: Addison-Wesley, 1978.

Campbell, J. *The Hero With a Thousand Faces.* (2nd ed.) Princeton, N.J.: Princeton University Press, 1968.

Campbell, J. *Myths to Live By.* New York: Bantam, 1972.

Carkhuff, R. R., and Berenson, B. G. *Beyond Counseling and Psychotherapy.* (2nd ed.) New York: Holt, Rinehart & Winston, 1977.

Chamberlain, L. "How to Be an Ericksonian (Milton, Not Erik)." In G. C. Ellenbogen (ed.), *The Primal Whimper.* New York: Guilford Press, 1989.

Chessick, R. D. *Great Ideas in Psychotherapy.* New York: Aronson, 1977.

Chessick, R. D. "Current Issues in Intensive Psychotherapy." *American Journal of Psychotherapy,* 1982, *36,* 438–449.

Corey, G. *Theory and Practice of Counseling and Psychotherapy.* (4th ed.) Pacific Grove, Calif.: Brooks/Cole, 1990.

Cormier, L. S. "Critical Incidents in Counselor Development: Themes and Patterns." *Journal of Counseling and Development,* 1988, *67,* 131–132.

Cornsweet, C. "Nonspecific Factors and Theoretical Choice." *Psychotherapy,* 1983, *20* (3), 307–313.

Craig, P. E. "Sanctuary and Presence: An Existential View of the Therapist's Contribution." *Humanistic Psychologist,* 1986, *14* (1), 22–28.

Dass, R. and Gorman, P. *How Can I Help? Stories and Reflections on Service.* New York: Knopf, 1985.

Decker, R. J. *Effective Psychotherapy: The Silent Dialogue.* New York: Hemisphere, 1988.

de Shazer, S. *Keys to Solution in Brief Therapy.* New York: Norton, 1985.

de Shazer, S. *Clues: Investigating Solutions in Brief Therapy.* New York: Norton, 1988.

DiGiuseppe, R. A. "Eclectic Uses of Metaphor in Therapy."

Paper presented at the 96th annual meeting of the American Psychological Association, Atlanta, 1988.

Dollard, J., and Auld, F. *Scoring Human Motives: A Manual.* New Haven: Yale University Press, 1959.

Dollard, J., and Miller, N. E. *Personality and Psychotherapy.* New York: McGraw-Hill, 1950.

Douglass, B., and Moustakas, C. "Heuristic Inquiry: The Internal Search to Know." *Journal of Humanistic Psychology,* 1985, *25* (3), 39–55.

Driscoll, R. H. *Pragmatic Psychotherapy.* New York: Van Nostrand Reinhold, 1984.

Dryden, W. "Eclectic Psychotherapies: A Critique of Leading Approaches." In J. C. Norcross (ed.), *Handbook of Eclectic Psychotherapy.* New York: Brunner/Mazel, 1986.

Duncan, B. L., Parks, M. B., and Rusk, G. S. "Eclectic Strategic Practice: A Process Constructive Perspective." *Journal of Marital and Family Therapy,* 1990, *16* (2), 165–178.

Dyer, W. W., and Vriend, J. *Counseling Techniques That Work.* New York: Funk & Wagnalls, 1975.

Egan, G. *The Skilled Helper.* Pacific Grove, Calif.: Brooks/Cole, 1990.

Elliott, R. "That in Your Hands: A Comprehensive Process Analysis of a Significant Event in Psychotherapy." *Psychiatry,* 1983, *46,* 113–129.

Ellis, A. *Overcoming Resistance.* New York: Springer, 1985.

Elstein, A. S. "Cognitive Processes in Clinical Inference and Decision Making." In D. C. Turk and P. Salovey (eds.), *Reasoning, Inference, and Judgment in Clinical Psychology.* New York: Free Press, 1988.

Erskine, R. G., and Moursand, J. P. *Integrative Psychotherapy in Action.* Newbury Park, Calif.: Sage, 1988.

Eysenck, H. J. "A Mish-Mash of Theories." *International Journal of Psychiatry.* 1970, *9,* 140–146.

Farber, B. A. "The Effects of Psychotherapeutic Practice upon Psychotherapists." *Psychotherapy.* 1983, *20,* 174–182.

Farber, B. A. "Clinical Psychologists' Perception of Psychotherapeutic Work." *Clinical Psychologist.* 1985a, *38,* 10–13.

Farber, B. A. "The Genesis, Development, and Implications

of Psychological-Mindedness in Psychologists." *Psychotherapy,* 1985b, *22* (2), 170–177.

Farber, B. A., and Heifetz, L. J. "The Satisfaction and Stress of Psychotherapeutic Work." *Professional Psychology.* 1981, *12,* 621–630.

Fensterheim, H., and Glazer, H. I. (eds.). *Behavioral Psychotherapy: Basic Principles and Case Studies in an Integrative Clinical Model.* New York: Brunner/Mazel, 1983.

Fiedler, F. E. "Comparison of Therapeutic Relationships in Psychoanalytic, Non-directive, and Adlerian Therapy." *Journal of Consulting Psychology,* 1951, *14,* 436–445.

Fisch, R., Weakland, J., and Segal, L. *The Tactics of Change: Doing Therapy Briefly.* San Francisco: Jossey-Bass, 1982.

Fish, J. M. *Placebo Therapy: A Practical Guide to Social Influence in Psychotherapy.* San Francisco: Jossey-Bass, 1973.

Frank, J. D. *Persuasion and Healing.* Baltimore: Johns Hopkins University Press, 1973.

Frank, J. D., and others. *Effective Ingredients of Successful Psychotherapy.* New York: Brunner/Mazel, 1978.

French, T. M. "Interrelations Between Psychoanalysis and the Experimental Work of Pavlov." *American Journal of Psychiatry.* 1933, *89,* 1165–1203.

Freud, S., *Therapy and Technique.* New York: Collier, 1963.

Fuhriman, A., Paul, S. C., and Burlingame, G. M. "Eclectic Time-Limited Therapy." In J. C. Norcross (ed.), *Handbook of Eclectic Psychotherapy.* New York: Brunner/Mazel, 1986.

Fulghum, R. *All I Really Need to Know I Learned in Kindergarten.* New York: Villard Books, 1988.

Gambrill, E. *Critical Thinking in Clinical Practice: Improving the Accuracy of Judgments and Decisions About Clients.* San Francisco: Jossey-Bass, 1990.

Garfield, S. L. "Research on Client Variables in Psychotherapy." In S. L. Garfield and A. E. Bergin (eds.), *Handbook of Psychotherapy and Behavior Change.* New York: Wiley, 1978.

Garfield, S. L. *Psychotherapy: An Eclectic Approach.* New York: Wiley, 1980.

Garfield, S. L. "An Eclectic Psychotherapy." In J. C. Norcross (ed.), *Handbook of Eclectic Psychotherapy.* New York: Brunner/Mazel, 1986.

Garfield, S. L., and Bergin, A. E. "Introduction and Historical Overview." In S. L. Garfield and A. E. Bergin (eds.), *Handbook of Psychotherapy and Behavior Change.* (3rd ed.) New York: Wiley, 1986.

Gauron, E. F., and Dickinson, J. K. "The Influence of Seeing the Patient First on Diagnostic Decision Making in Psychiatry." *American Journal of Psychiatry,* 1969, *126,* 199–205.

Gazda, G., and others. *Human Relations Development.* Boston: Allyn & Bacon, 1977.

Gilbert, P., Hughes, W., and Dryden, W. "The Therapist as Crucial Variable in Psychotherapy." In W. Dryden and L. Spurling (eds.), *On Becoming a Psychotherapist.* London: Tavistock/Routledge, 1989.

Glantz, K., and Pearce, J. K. *Exiles from Eden: Psychotherapy from an Evolutionary Perspective.* New York: Norton, 1989.

Gold, J. R. "The Integration of Psychoanalytic, Cognitive, and Interpersonal Approaches in the Psychotherapy of Borderline and Narcissistic Disorders." *Journal of Integrative and Eclectic Psychotherapy,* 1990, *9* (1), 49–68.

Goldberg, C. *On Being a Psychotherapist: The Journey of the Healer.* New York: Gardner, 1986.

Goldberg, P. *The Intuitive Edge.* Los Angeles: Tarcher, 1983.

Goldfried, M. R. "Resistance and Clinical Behavior Therapy." In P. L. Wachtel (ed.), *Resistance: Psychodynamic and Behavioral Approaches.* New York: Plenum Press, 1982a.

Goldfried, M. R. (ed.). *Converging Themes in Psychotherapy.* New York: Springer, 1982b.

Goldfried, M. R., and Davidson, G. *Clinical Behavior Therapy.* New York: Holt, Rinehart & Winston, 1976.

Goldfried, M. R., and Newman, C. "Psychotherapy Integration: An Historical Perspective." In J. C. Norcross (ed.), *Handbook of Eclectic Psychotherapy.* New York: Brunner/Mazel, 1986.

Gomez, E. A., and O'Connell, W. E. "Re-viewing the Initial Interview." *Journal of Integrative and Eclectic Psychotherapy,* 1987, *6* (1), 32–36.

Gottman, J. M., and Lieblum, S. R. *How To Do Psychotherapy and How to Evaluate It.* New York: Holt, Rinehart & Winston, 1974.

Greenberg, L. S., and Pinsof, W. M. (eds.). *The Therapeutic Process: A Research Handbook.* New York: Guilford Press, 1986.

Gurman, A. S., and Razin, M. (eds.). *Effective Psychotherapy: A Handbook of Research.* Elmsford, N.Y.: Pergamon Press, 1977.

Guy, J. D. *The Personal Life of the Psychotherapist.* New York: Wiley, 1987.

Haley, J. *Ordeal Therapy: Unusual Ways to Change Behavior.* San Francisco: Jossey-Bass, 1984.

Haley, J. "Interminable Therapy." In J. Zeig and S. Gilligan (eds.), *Brief Therapy: Myths, Methods, and Metaphors.* New York: Brunner/Mazel, 1990.

Harper, R. A. "Helping People to Enjoy Life." *Humanistic Psychologist,* 1985, *13* (2), 10.

Hart, J. T. *Modern Eclectic Therapy.* New York: Plenum, 1983.

Hayward, J. W. *Perceiving Ordinary Magic: Science and Intuitive Wisdom.* Boulder, Colo.: New Science Library, 1984.

Held, B. S. "Towards a Strategic Eclecticism." *Psychotherapy,* 1984, *21,* 232–241.

Henry, W., Sims, J., and Spray, S. L. *Public and Private Lives of Psychotherapists.* San Francisco: Jossey-Bass, 1973.

Herink, R. (ed.). *The Psychotherapy Handbook.* New York: New American Library, 1980.

Hilgard, E. R., and Bower, G. H. *Theories of Learning.* Englewood Cliffs, N.J.: Prentice-Hall, 1975.

Hobbs, N. "Sources of Gain in Psychotherapy." *American Psychologist,* 1962, *17,* 740–747.

Howard, G. S., Nance, D. W., and Myers, P. "Adaptive Counseling and Therapy: An Integrative, Eclectic Model." *The Counseling Psychologist,* 1986, *14* (3), 363–442.

Ivey, A. *Microcounseling: Innovations in Interviewing Training.* Springfield, Ill.: Thomas, 1971.

James, W. *Pragmatism.* New York: New American Library, 1907.

Jaspers, K. *The Nature of Psychotherapy.* Chicago: University of Chicago Press, 1963.

Jensen, J. P., Bergin, A. E., and Greaves, D. W. "The Meaning of Eclecticism." *Professional Psychology,* 1990, *21* (2), 124–130.

Johnson, C., and Connors, M. E. *The Etiology and Treatment of*

Bulimia Nervosa: A Biopsychosocial Perspective. New York: Basic Books, 1989.

Jung, C. G. *Memories, Dreams, Reflections.* New York: Vintage Books, 1961.

Kagan, N., and Schauble, P. G. "Affect Simulation in Interpersonal Process Recall." *Journal of Counseling Psychology,* 1969, *16,* 309–313.

Kahn, E. "Heinz Kohut and Carl Rogers: Toward a Constructive Collaboration." *Psychotherapy,* 1989, *26* (4), 427–435.

Kanfer, F. H., and Goldstein, A. P. (eds.). *Helping People Change.* (3rd ed.) Elmsford, N.Y.: Pergamon Press, 1986.

Kanfer, F. H., and Schefft, B. K. *Guiding the Process of Therapeutic Change.* Champaign, Ill.: Research Press, 1988.

Kaplan, H. S. *The New Sex Therapy.* New York: Brunner/Mazel, 1974.

Karasu, T. B. "The Specificity Versus Nonspecificity Dilemma: Toward Identifying Therapeutic Change Agents." *American Journal of Psychiatry,* 1986, *143* (6), 687–695.

Kazdin, A. E. "The Evaluation of Psychotherapy: Research Design and Methodology." In S. L. Garfield and A. E. Bergin (eds.), *Handbook of Psychotherapy and Behavior Change.* (3rd ed.) New York: Wiley, 1986.

Koestler, A. *The Act of Creation.* New York: Dell, 1964.

Kohut, H. *The Analysis of the Self.* New York: International Universities Press, 1971.

Konstantareas, M. M. "A Psychoeducational Model for Working with Families of Autistic Children." *Journal of Marital and Family Therapy,* 1990, *16* (1), 59–70.

Kottler, J. A. *Pragmatic Group Leadership.* Pacific Grove, Calif.: Brooks/Cole, 1983.

Kottler, J. A. *On Being a Therapist.* San Francisco: Jossey-Bass, 1986.

Kottler, J. A., and Blau, D. S. *The Imperfect Therapist: Learning from Failure in Therapeutic Practice.* San Francisco: Jossey-Bass, 1989.

Kramer, S. A. *Positive Endings in Psychotherapy: Bringing Meaningful Closure to Therapeutic Relationships.* San Francisco: Jossey-Bass, 1990.

Kroll, J. *The Challenge of the Borderline Patient.* New York: Norton, 1988.

Kubie, L. S. "Relation of the Conditioned Reflex to Psychoanalytic Technique." *Archives of Neurology and Psychiatry,* 1934, *32,* 1137–1142.

Kuhn, T. S. *The Structure of Scientific Revolutions.* Chicago: University of Chicago Press, 1962.

Kupers, T. *Ending Therapy: The Meaning of Termination.* New York: New York University Press, 1988.

Lafferty, P., Beutler, L. E., and Crago, M. "Differences Between More and Less Effective Psychotherapists: A Study of Select Therapist Variables." *Journal of Consulting and Clinical Psychology,* 1989, *57* (1), 76–80.

Lambert, M. J. "Some Implications of Psychotherapy Outcome Research for Eclectic Psychotherapy." *International Journal of Eclectic Psychotherapy,* 1986, *5* (1), 16–44.

Lambert, M. J., Shapiro, D. A., and Bergin, A. E. "The Effectiveness of Psychotherapy." In S. L. Garfield and A. E. Bergin (eds.), *Handbook of Psychotherapy and Behavior Change.* (3rd ed.) New York: Wiley, 1986.

Langs, R. *Resistances and Interventions: The Nature of Therapeutic Work.* New York: Jason Aronson, 1981.

Lazarus, A. A. *Multimodal Behavior Therapy.* New York: Springer, 1976.

Lazarus, A. A. *The Practice of Multimodal Therapy.* New York: McGraw-Hill, 1981.

Lazarus, A. A. (ed.). *Casebook of Multimodal Therapy.* New York: Guilford Press, 1985.

Lazarus, A. A. "The Need for Technical Eclecticism." In J. K. Zeig (ed.) *The Evolution of Psychotherapy.* New York: Brunner/Mazel, 1986.

Lazarus, A. A. "Invited Address: Can Psychotherapists Transcend the Shackles of Their Training?" Paper presented at the 97th annual meeting of the American Psychological Association, New Orleans, 1989.

Leerhsen, C. "Unite and Conquer." *Newsweek,* Feb. 5, 1990, pp. 50–55.

Legge, J. *The Chinese Classics.* Fairlawn, N.J.: Oxford University Press, 1935.

Lindbergh, A. M. *Gift from the Sea.* New York: Random House, 1955.

Linehan, M. M. "Perspectives on the Interpersonal Relationship in Behavior Therapy." *Journal of Integrative and Eclectic Psychotherapy,* 1988, *7* (3), 278–290.

London, P. *The Modes and Morals of Psychotherapy.* New York: Holt, Rinehart & Winston, 1964.

London, P. "Major Issues in Psychotherapy Integration." *International Journal of Eclectic Psychotherapy,* 1986, *5* (3), 211–217.

London, P. "Metamorphosis in Psychotherapy: Slouching Toward Integration." *Journal of Integrative and Eclectic Psychotherapy,* 1988, *7* (1), 3–12.

Long, L., Paradise, L. V., and Long, T. J. *Questionning.* Pacific Grove, Calif.: Brooks/Cole, 1981.

Luborsky, L., and others. "Factors Influencing the Outcome of Psychotherapy." *Psychological Bulletin,* 1971, *75,* 145–185.

Luborsky, L., Singer, B., and Luborsky, L. "Comparative Studies of Psychotherapy." *Archives of General Psychiatry,* 1975, *32,* 995–1008.

Luborsky, L., and others. "Do Therapists Vary Much in Their Success?" *American Journal of Orthopsychiatry,* 1986, *56* (4), 501–512.

Luks, A. "Helper's High." *Psychology Today,* Oct. 1988, pp. 39–42.

Madanes, C. *Strategic Family Therapy.* San Francisco: Jossey-Bass, 1981.

Madanes, C. "Advances in Strategic Therapy." In J. K. Zeig (ed.), *The Evolution of Psychotherapy.* New York: Brunner/Mazel, 1986.

Mahrer, A. R. *The Integration of Psychotherapies.* New York: Human Sciences Press, 1989.

Mahrer, A. R., and Nadler, W. P. "Good Moments in Psychotherapy: A Preliminary Review, a List, and Some Promising Research Avenues." *Journal of Consulting and Clinical Psychology,* 1986, *54* (1), 10–15.

Marmor, J. "Dynamic Psychotherapy and Behavior Therapy: Are They Irreconcilable?" *Archives of General Psychiatry,* 1971, *24,* 22–28.

Marmor, J. "Common Operational Factors in Diverse Approaches." In A. Burton (ed.), *What Makes Behavior Change Possible?* New York: Brunner/Mazel, 1976.

Marmor, J. "The Psychotherapeutic Process: Common Denominators in Diverse Approaches." In J. K. Zeig (ed.), *The Evolution of Psychotherapy*. New York: Brunner/Mazel, 1986.

Marmor, J., and Woods, S. M. (eds.). *The Interface Between Psychodynamic and Behavioral Therapists*. New York: Plenum, 1980.

Marston, A. R. "What Makes Therapists Run? A Model for Analysis of Motivational Styles." *Psychotherapy*, 1984, *21*, 456–459.

Maruyama, M. "Heterogenistics: An Epistemological Restructuring of Biological and Social Sciences." *Acta Biotheretica*, 1977, *26*, 120–137.

Masterson, J. F. *Countertransference and Psychotherapeutic Technique*. New York: Brunner/Mazel, 1983.

Matarazzo, R. G., and Patterson, D. "Research on the Teaching and Learning of Therapeutic Skills." In S. L. Garfield and A. E. Bergin (eds.), *Handbook of Psychotherapy and Behavior Change*. (3rd ed.) New York: Wiley, 1986.

May, R. *The Discovery of Being*. New York: Norton, 1983.

May, R. "Therapy in Our Day." In J. K. Zeig (ed.), *The Evolution of Psychotherapy*. New York: Brunner/Mazel, 1986.

Messer, S. B. "Eclecticism in Psychotherapy: Underlying Assumptions, Problems, and Trade-offs." In J. C. Norcross (ed.), *Handbook of Eclectic Psychotherapy*. New York: Brunner/Mazel, 1986.

Messer, S. B. "Psychoanalytic Perspectives on the Therapist-Client Relationship." *Journal of Integrative and Eclectic Psychotherapy*, 1988, *7* (3), 268–277.

Millon, T. "Personologic Psychotherapy: Ten Commandments for a Posteclectic Approach to Integrative Treatment." *Psychotherapy*, 1988, *25* (2), 209–219.

Minuchin, S. "My Many Voices." In J. K. Zeig (ed.), *The Evolution of Psychotherapy*. New York: Brunner/Mazel, 1986.

Moustakas, C. *Rhythms, Rituals, and Relationships*. Detroit: Center for Humanistic Studies, 1981.

Moustakas, C. "Being in, Being for, and Being with." *Humanistic Psychologist*, 1986, *14* (2), 100–104.

Moustakas, C. *Phenomenology, Science, and Psychotherapy*. University College of Cape Breton, 1988.

Murgatroyd, S., and Apter, M. J. "A Structural-Phenomenological Approach to Eclectic Psychotherapy." In J. C. Norcross (ed.), *Handbook of Eclectic Psychotherapy*. New York: Brunner/Mazel, 1986.

Napier, A. Y. *The Fragile Bond*. New York: Harper & Row, 1988.

Norcross, J. C. Preface. In J. C. Norcross (ed.), *Handbook of Eclectic Psychotherapy*. New York: Brunner/Mazel, 1986.

Norcross, J. C., and Grencavage, L. M. "Eclecticism and Integration in Counselling and Psychotherapy: Major Themes and Obstacles." *British Journal of Guidance and Counselling*, 1989, *17* (3), 227–247.

Norcross, J. C., and Napolitano, G. "Defining Our Journal and Ourselves." *International Journal of Eclectic Psychotherapy*, 1986, *5* (3), 249–255.

Norcross, J. C., and Prochaska, J. "A National Survey of Clinical Psychologists: Affiliations and Orientations." *Clinical Psychologist*, 1982, *35* (3), 4–6.

Norcross, J. C., Strausser, M. S., and Faltus, F. J. "The Therapist's Therapist." *American Journal of Psychotherapy*, 1988, *42* (1), 53–66.

O'Hanlon, W. H. "Debriefing Myself." *Family Therapy Networker*, Mar. 1990, pp. 48–69.

O'Hanlon, W. H., and Weiner-Davis, M. *In Search of Solutions: A New Direction in Psychotherapy*. New York: Norton, 1989.

Omer, H. "Therapeutic Impact: A Nonspecific Major Factor in Directive Psychotherapies." *Psychotherapy*, 1987, *24* (1), 52–57.

Omer, H., and London, P. "Metamorphosis in Psychotherapy: End of the Systems Era." *Psychotherapy*, 1988, *25* (2), 171–180.

Orlinsky, D. E., and Howard, K. I. "The Therapist's Experience of Psychotherapy." In A. S. Gurman and A. M. Razin (eds.), *Effective Psychotherapy: A Handbook of Research*, Elmsford, N.Y.: Pergamon Press, 1977.

Orlinsky, D. E., and Howard, K. I. "Process Outcome in Psychotherapy." In S. L. Garfield and A. E. Bergin (eds.), *Handbook of Psychotherapy and Behavior Change*. (3rd ed.) New York: Wiley, 1986.

Orne, M. T., and Wender, P. H. "Anticipatory Socialization

for Psychotherapy: Method and Rationale." *American Journal of Psychiatry,* 1968, *124,* 1202–1212.

Palmer, J. O. *A Primer of Eclectic Psychotherapy.* Pacific Grove, Calif.: Brooks/Cole, 1980.

Parloff, M. B., Waskow, I. E., and Wolfe, B. E. "Research on Therapist Variables in Relation to Process and Outcome." In A. E. Bergin and S. L. Garfield (eds.), *Handbook of Psychotherapy and Behavior Change.* (2nd ed.) New York: Wiley, 1978.

Patterson, C. H. *Theories of Counseling and Psychotherapy.* (3rd ed.) New York: Harper & Row, 1980.

Patterson, C. H. "Foundations for an Eclectic Psychotherapy." *Psychotherapy,* 1989, *26* (4), 427–435.

Peck, M. *The Road Less Traveled.* New York: Simon & Schuster, 1978.

Pentony, P. *Models of Influence in Psychotherapy.* New York: Free Press, 1981.

Polanyi, M. *The Tacit Dimension.* Garden City, N.Y.: Doubleday, 1967.

Pope, B. "Research of Therapeutic Style." In A. S. Gurman and A. M. Razin (eds.), *Effective Psychotherapy: A Handbook of Research.* Elmsford, N.Y.: Pergamon Press, 1977.

Pope, K. S., Tabachnick, B. G., and Keith-Spiegel, P. "Good and Poor Practices in Psychotherapy: National Survey of Beliefs of Psychologists." *Professional Psychology,* 1988, *19* (5), 547–552.

Prochaska, J. O. *Systems of Psychotherapy: A Transtheoretical Approach.* (2nd ed.) Homewood, Ill.: Dorsey Press, 1984.

Prochaska, J. O., and DiClemente, C. C. *The Transtheoretical Approach: Crossing the Traditional Boundaries of Therapy.* Homewood, Ill.: Dow Jones-Irwin, 1984a.

Prochaska, J. O. and DiClemente, C. C. "Transtheoretical Therapy: Toward an Integrative Model of Change." *Psychotherapy,* 1984b, *19,* 276–288.

Rice, L. N., and Greenberg, L. S. "The New Research Paradigm." In L. N. Rice and L. S. Greenberg (eds.), *Patterns of Change.* New York: Guilford Press, 1984.

Rice, L. N., and Saperia, E. P. "Task Analysis of the Resolution of Problematic Reactions." In L. N. Rice and L. S. Greenberg (eds.), *Patterns of Change.* New York: Guilford Press, 1984.

Rice, L. N., and Wagstaff, A. K. "Client Voice Quality and Expressive Style as Indices of Productive Psychotherapy." *Journal of Consulting Psychology,* 1967, *31,* 557–563.

Richert, A. "Differential Prescriptions for Psychotherapy on the Basis of Client Role Preferences." *Psychotherapy: Theory, Research, and Practice,* 1983, *20,* 321–329.

Rogers, C. R. *Counseling and Psychotherapy.* Boston: Houghton-Mifflin, 1942.

Rogers, C. R. "Person or Science? A Philosophical Question." *American Psychologist,* 1955, *10,* 267–278.

Rogers, C. R. "The Necessary and Sufficient Conditions of Therapeutic Change." *Journal of Consulting Psychology,* 1957, *21,* 95–103.

Rogers, C. R. "Rogers, Kohut, and Erickson." In J. K. Zeig (ed.) *The Evolution of Psychotherapy.* New York: Brunner/Mazel, 1986.

Rosenzweig, S. "Some Implicit Common Factors in Diverse Methods in Psychotherapy." *American Journal of Orthopsychiatry,* 1936, *6,* 412–415.

Rossi, E. L. "Psychological Shocks and Creative Moments in Psychotherapy." *American Journal of Clinical Hypnosis,* 1973, *16* (1), 9–22.

Rothenberg, A. *The Creative Process of Psychotherapy.* New York: Norton, 1988.

Russell, B. *The Problems of Philosophy.* London: Oxford University Press, 1959. (Originally published 1912.)

Ryan, V. L., and Gizynski, M. N. "Behavior Therapy in Retrospect: Patients' Feelings About Their Behavior Therapists." *Journal of Consulting and Clinical Psychology,* 1971, *37,* 1–9.

Salovey, P., and Turk, D. C. "Some Effects of Mood on Clinician's Memory." In D. C. Turk and P. Salovey (eds.), *Reasoning, Inference, and Judgment in Clinical Psychology.* New York: Free Press, 1988.

Sammons, M. T., and Gravitz, M. A. "Theoretical Orientation of Professional Psychologists and Their Former Professors." *Professional Psychology,* 1990, *21* (2), 131–134.

Sandifer, M. G., Hordern, A., and Green, L. M. "The Psychiatric Interview: The Impact of the First Three Minutes." *American Journal of Psychiatry,* 1970, *126,* 968–973.

Schein, E. H. "Personal Change Through Interpersonal Relationships." In W. G. Bennis, D. W. Berlew, E. H. Schein, and F. I. Steele (eds.), *Interpersonal Dynamics: Essays and Readings in Human Interaction.* (3rd ed.) Homewood, Ill.: Dorsey Press, 1973.

Schön, D. A. *The Reflective Practitioner.* New York: Basic Books, 1983.

Seligman, M. E. P. *Helplessness: On Depression, Development, and Death.* San Francisco: Freeman, 1975.

Shands, H. *Thinking and Psychotherapy.* Cambridge, Mass.: Harvard University Press, 1960.

Singer, P. *The Expanding Circle: Ethics and Sociobiology.* New York: New American Library, 1981.

Sloane, R. B., and others. *Psychotherapy Versus Behavior Therapy.* Cambridge, Mass.: Harvard University Press, 1975.

Snyder, M., and Thomsen, C. J. "Interaction Between Therapists and Clients: Hypothesis Testing and Behavioral Confirmation." In D. C. Turk and P. Salovey (eds.), *Reasoning, Inference, and Judgment in Clinical Psychology.* New York: Free Press, 1988.

Spence, D. P. *Narrative Truth and Historical Truth.* New York: Norton, 1982.

Steinlin, H., and Weber, G., *Unlocking the Family Door: A Systematic Approach to the Understanding and Treatment of Anorexia Nervosa.* New York: Brunner/Mazel, 1989.

Stiles, W. B., Shapiro, D. A., and Elliott, R. "Are All Psychotherapies Equivalent?" *American Psychologist,* 1986, *41* (2), 165–180.

Strupp, H. S. "On the Basic Ingredients of Psychotherapy." *Journal of Consulting and Clinical Psychology,* 1973, *41* (1), 1–8.

Strupp, H. S. "A Reformulation of the Dynamics of the Therapist's Contribution." In A. S. Gurman and A. M. Razin (eds.), *Effective Psychotherapy: A Handbook of Research.* Elmsford, N.Y.: Pergamon Press, 1977.

Strupp, H. S. "Invited Address: A Little Bit of Bad Process Can Go a Long Way in Psychotherapy," American Psychological Association Convention, New Orleans, 1989.

Sundland, D. M. "Theoretical Orientations of Psychotherapists." In A. S. Gurman and A. M. Razin (eds.), *Effective Psychotherapy: A Handbook of Research.* Elmsford, N.Y.: Pergamon Press, 1977.

Thorne, F. C. *The Principles of Personal Counseling.* Brandon, Vt.: *Journal of Clinical Psychology Press,* 1950.

Thorne, F. C. "Eclectic Psychotherapy." In R. Corsini (ed.), *Current Psychotherapies.* Itasca, Ill.: Peacock, 1973.

Truax, C. B. "Reinforcement and Nonreinforcement in Rogerian Psychotherapy." *Journal of Abnormal Psychology,* 1966, *71,* 1-9.

Truax, C. B., and Carkhuff, R. R. *Toward Effective Counseling and Psychotherapy.* Chicago: Aldine, 1967.

Tryon, G. S. "The Pleasures and Displeasures of Full Time Private Practice." *Clinical Psychologist,* 1983, *36,* 45-48.

Turk, D. C., and Salovey, P. "Clinical Information Processing: Bias Inoculation." In R. Ingram (ed.), *Information Processing Approaches to Psychopathology and Clinical Psychology.* New York: Academic Press, 1986.

Wachtel, P. *Psychoanalysis and Behavior Therapy: Toward an Integration.* New York: Basic Books, 1977.

Walsh, B. M., and Peterson, L. E. "Philosophical Foundations of Psychological Theory: The Issue of Synthesis." *Psychotherapy,* 1985, *22* (2), 145-153.

Walsh, B. M., and Rosen, P. M. *Self-Mutilation: Theory, Research, and Treatment.* New York: Guilford Press, 1988.

Washton, A. M. *Cocaine Addiction: Treatment, Recovery, and Relapse Prevention.* New York: Norton, 1989.

Watzlawick, P. "If You Desire to See, Learn How To Act." In J. K. Zeig (ed.), *The Evolution of Psychotherapy.* New York: Brunner/Mazel, 1986.

Watzlawick, P., Weakland, J. H., and Fisch, R. *Change: Principles of Problem Formation and Problem Resolution.* New York: Norton, 1974.

Weinberg, G. *The Heart of Psychotherapy.* New York: St. Martin's Press, 1984.

Weiner-Davis, M. "In Praise of Solutions." *Family Therapy Networker,* Mar. 1990, pp. 43–66.

Welles, J. F. *The Story of Stupidity.* Orient, N. Y.: Mt. Pleasant Press, 1988.

Whitaker, C. A. "The Dynamics of the American Family as Deduced From 20 Years of Family Therapy." In J. K. Zeig (ed.), *The Evolution of Psychotherapy.* New York: Brunner/Mazel, 1986.

White, G. D., and Pollard, J. "Assessing Therapeutic Competence from Therapy Session Attendance." *Professional Psychology,* 1982, *13,* 628–633.

Wogan, M., and Norcross, J. C. "Dimensions of Therapeutic Skills and Techniques." *Psychotherapy,* 1985, *22* (1), 63–74.

Wolberg, L. R. "Discussion of Mind/Body Communication and the New Language of Human Facilitation." In J. K. Zeig (ed.), *The Evolution of Psychotherapy.* New York: Brunner/Mazel, 1986.

Wolfe, B. E. "Phobias, Panic, and Psychotherapy Integration." *Journal of Integrative and Eclectic Psychotherapy,* 1989, *8* (3), 264–276.

Wolpe, J., and Lazarus, A. *Behavior Therapy Techniques.* Elmsford, N.Y.: Pergamon Press, 1966.

Woody, R. H. *Psychobehavioral Counseling and Therapy: Integrating Behavioral and Insight Techniques.* New York: Appleton-Century-Crofts, 1971.

Wylie, M. S. "Brief Therapy on the Couch." *Family Therapy Networker,* Mar. 1990, pp. 26–66.

Yalom, I. D. *Existential Psychotherapy.* New York: Basic Books, 1980.

Yalom, I. D. *Love's Executioner and Other Tales of Psychotherapy.* New York: Basic Books, 1989.

Zeig, J. K. "The Evolution of Psychotherapy—Fundamental Issues." In J. K. Zeig (ed.) *The Evolution of Psychotherapy.* New York: Brunner/Mazel, 1986.

Zukav, G. *The Dancing Wu Li Masters.* New York: Bantam Books, 1979.

Index